# Delivering Effective Virtual Presentations

# Delivering Effective Virtual Presentations

K. Virginia Hemby

BUSINESS EXPERT PRESS

First published in 2020 by
Business Expert Press, LLC
222 East 46th Street, New York, NY 10017
www.businessexpertpress.com

ISBN-13: 978-1-63157-967-7 (paperback)
ISBN-13: 978-1-63157-968-4 (e-book)

Business Expert Press Corporate Communication Collection

Collection ISSN: 2156-8162 (print)
Collection ISSN: 2156-8170 (electronic)

Cover and interior design by S4Carlisle Publishing Services Private Ltd., Chennai, India
Cover image licensed by Ingram Image, StockPhotoSecrets.com

First edition: 2020

10 9 8 7 6 5 4 3 2 1

Printed in the United States of America.

# Abstract

The virtual environment has led to opportunities that previously existed only in real time and at on-site locations. For example, the advent of GoToMeeting, WebEx, Google Hangouts, YouTube, TED Talks, and many other platforms has transformed the way in which we meet, present, and interact. However, the way in which students are instructed to create and deliver presentations, to plan and prepare for meetings, and to seek and participate in training has not altered—or in the best of circumstances has received only minimal attention. In fact, oral presentation instruction in most classes still follows the traditional speech-making (or formal address) approach for teaching students the concepts of creating and delivering effective presentations.

Organizations have recognized the impact of web conferences and virtual meetings to their bottom line. However, their employees have learned how to navigate the virtual environment for presentations and meetings through trial and error. Numerous training and consulting groups have created guides for different areas of the virtual presentation. Companies who market the various platforms and tools also offer assistance with training (user documentation or guides) for the technology. *Delivering Effective Virtual Presentations* offers these individuals a user-friendly method to fill the gap between their existing knowledge, skills, and abilities, and those necessary for the virtual presentation environment.

In a world driven by technology, the absence of instructional guides and materials for the "how-to" of delivering effective virtual presentations must be addressed. This book provides a practical approach with clear guidelines for creating and delivering webinars, e-meetings, virtual presentations, and virtual product demonstrations, including checklists and examples. Whether you are a college student, an employee, or a supervisor/manager/executive, this book will provide you with the knowledge and tools needed to be an effective virtual presenter.

# Keywords

virtual presentations; e-meetings; webinars; professional speaking; virtual communication skills; teaching virtual presentation skills

# Contents

# Acknowledgments

Thanking the people in your life who have helped you develop into the person you are can be very difficult. You do not want to forget anyone and are just sure that you will no matter how hard you try. I owe a debt of gratitude to my husband, Dr Skip Grubb, for his infinite patience and love. He has been my rock for 25 years through an accident that resulted in my traumatic brain injury and lingering deficits—including a personality change. He likes to tell people he has been married to two different women with the same name. You have to love him! My parents, James and Fannie Hemby, are where my story begins. They taught me that hard work and perseverance can get you a long way. I am fortunate to still have both parents. My dad thinks my inability to control what I think and say is humorous. Brain injuries often take away your governor, that device that resembles the brake in your car. For me, if I think it, I say it—no governor between the brain and the mouth. I'm glad James Hemby thinks I'm funny. He's my dad, so what he thinks should matter. My son, Matthew, and his sweet family—his wife, Kaiti, and my three grandsons—Benson, Cash, and Tucker, to whom I am GiGi—are my life's greatest blessings.

Finally, I would like to thank my students. I may not be able to re-member every name, but I have your faces in my memory. I often wonder where you are and how you are faring. You have taught me more than you know. I wish I could list each of you here because you deserve recognition for the smiles, grimaces, laughter, groans, and a few choice words that you brought to me or brought out in me! I believe you are all out there conquering the world and hope that you truly succeed or have succeeded in whatever you chose to do with your life.

# CHAPTER 1

# What Are Virtual Presentations?

In 2011, the American Management Association (AMA) posted an article titled "Perfect Your Virtual Presentations." This article encapsulated an interview conducted by AMA's podcast program, Edgewise, of Roger Courville, author of *The Virtual Presenter's Handbook*. Courville discussed the process for an electronic presentation and how it differs from that of a traditional presentation. In his closing remarks, Courville stated that he was working on a special program on virtual presentations for AMA and that it should launch in August of that same year. He stated, "Increasingly, executives and managers will be asked to use the new technology and deliver virtual presentations. And they will need to perfect the skills this will demand" (AMA Staff 2011).

Fast-forward almost a decade to 2020. Using the browser of your choice, conduct a search at the AMA website for anything related to presentations or building presentation skills, and you find no mention of virtual presentation skills—only traditional presentations. You find reference to virtual teams—leading, coaching, and being a successful member of—and the virtual trainer who delivers live online training. Again, though, no mention of developing skills for a virtual presenter (American Management Association 2019). Review any business communication textbook and you will likely find a mention of preparation required for virtual presentations. However, that mention is often buried in the chapter related to developing effective presentation skills whose content largely focuses on traditional presentations.

What changed? Did the AMA fail to see a definite need for developing virtual presentation skills? Do textbook authors feel that developing traditional presentation skills is more important than the ancillary skills needed for online presentations? Perhaps. Perhaps not. We could hypothesize that most people believe if we learn and develop the basic presentation skills, then those skills can easily be translated to the virtual environment. This same belief often underlies the request of administration to faculty when telling them to create and deliver more online courses and giving them a month to make it happen. "If you can create and teach a course in the traditional environment, then you just simply take that course material and adapt it to the online environment"—always an easier said than done mandate and certainly a process that takes longer than a month.

Before we move forward in our journey toward the goal of creating and delivering effective virtual presentations, we must first explain what we mean by virtual presentation.

## The Definition of Virtual Presentations

Defining virtual presentation is not as easy as you might expect. Asking a search engine to find the definition of virtual presentation may result in a list of links that tell you how to create a virtual presentation or that define a virtual event but none of which actually explain what a virtual presentation is. You might suppose that authorities on the subject expect that we can surmise the meaning of virtual presentation from the plethora of examples, software programs, meeting platforms, and conversations about them. However, are they presupposing that we will look at the broad picture or merely discuss them in terms of the definition of a presentation by way of a virtual environment?

For purposes of this book, we will define virtual presentations in the broader sense, as a component of virtual events.

---

Meetings Today defines a virtual event as "an occurrence of people gathering together where some or all of the attendees are not physically in the same location but are connected in a common environment. The common environment might be one of many types but is usually enabled through the use of computers and the Internet" (*Meetings Today* 2013).

Virtual presentations occur as part of a virtual event, whether scheduled as a synchronous webinar, a meeting, or a speech and, therefore, must be discussed from that perspective.

As with anything involving speeches and presentations, you will find that those occurring in the virtual environment also have their advantages and disadvantages. In the next portion of this chapter, we will review the benefits and the downsides to virtual presentations.

## Benefits of Virtual Presentations

If you look objectively at the advent of virtual presentations, you could say that they began when television became a staple in the home and broadcast networks aired news segments. Individual broadcasters reported the news of the day in real time prompting many to believe that if the viewer watching the news program could see the individual broadcasters live on the air, then those broadcasters could likewise see the viewer. People would dress up to watch television because they believed the individuals on the television programs could see them, the viewers. So, the viewers wanted to look nice for them. At that juncture in our history, we can definitively say that was not the case; however, the advent of virtual platforms, smartphones, and other technologies now make some of that scenario possible.

Those of us of a certain age can remember the television cartoon series, *The Jetsons*, and the videophone that was introduced in that show. Characters heard the ring of the videophone and saw the caller on the screen. In fact, Jane Jetson was seen talking with her mother via the videophone in the first episode of the series when it aired in 1962 (Novak 2013). You read that correctly—1962. However, the first videophone—outside of fictional television programs—was physically presented to the public at the 1964 New York World's Fair when Bell Telephone's Picturephone went on display (Darlin 2014). Despite the hype, the videophone never reached the height of popularity anticipated.

Having traversed more than five decades since that much hyped debut, we know that the videophone in its original design did not survive. However, the idea behind the videophone never disappeared. The concept merely evolved into an embedded application that is part of our smartphones, tablets, and computers (Novak 2013). Today, we use our devices as the conduit for video chatting, meeting, training, and presenting—activities the original developers of the Picturephone most likely never imagined.

In fact, if you think of the way meetings, conferences, training, and sales calls were handled a mere two decades ago, you can see how far we have traveled; we can only guess at what the next decades will bring. The first mobile phones were available for sale to consumers in 1994. The first cell phone was created by IBM—dubbed the Simon Personal Communicator—and had a monochrome display, a battery life of 1 hour, and limited features. The cost of the Simon Personal Communicator was $1,100. This phone was used primarily to make phone calls, although it had e-mail capability.

The first iteration of the iPhone was introduced by Steve Jobs in 2007. This version of the mobile phone changed the complexion of the industry. Enhanced features were available with the iPhone, including web browsing and searching. Battery life allowed for 8 hours of talk time and 250 hours of standby. The cost of the iPhone averaged $499 to $599, depending on the memory size selected by the consumer, a far cry from the cost of the Simon Personal Communicator (Owen 2018).

Between 2007 and 2019, advances in technology led to additional features being added to smartphones, escalated competition among competitors, and a proliferation in the use of smartphones across all demographics. In its 2018 report, the Pew Research Center revealed that 95 percent of Americans owned a smartphone of some type, up from its 2011 initial study findings that showed ownership to be at 35 percent (Pew Research Center: Internet and Technology 2018). The growth in the use of smartphones brought about another advancement—the development of applications designed to work specifically with the phones' operating systems to allow users to participate in meetings, take online courses, conduct research, play games, read books, maintain a social network presence, manage exercise, and many other activities too numerous to include. These apps and the additional capabilities of advanced smartphones have led to the devices being deemed replacements for computers.

Nonetheless, many still use computers and/or tablets to access virtual events. Companies that created applications for smartphones also have a similar or identical presence on the Internet. Platforms for virtual meetings, webinars, training, and learning can easily be accessed and used. Thus, when planning for virtual events, you must also consider the types of devices that participants may employ for those meetings, presentations, or training sessions.

Now that we have had a brief review of the development of technology and its impact on the proliferation of virtual events, we must delve into the benefits of those events for individuals, businesses, and educational institutions.

> The benefits of virtual events are extensive, reaching beyond the most obvious—a reduction in travel costs—to the less obvious—the myriad of opportunities available to us because of virtual events.

The following is not an all-inclusive list of benefits for virtual events as we are dealing with continually evolving technologies and platforms. We need to consider only artificial intelligence to hypothesize how the future of virtual events will be further impacted as that technology continues to expand. Therefore, presenting a list of every benefit of virtual events is simply not possible. We can, however, offer an overview of the main benefits.

- Save costs for both participants and organizers
- Increase participation in meetings, conferences, and training sessions
- Complement in-person events
- Create new value and opportunities to strengthen your brand
- Track and create custom reports based on the available resources of the platform you choose for your virtual events
- Access subject matter experts
- Spend less time traveling—or away from job responsibilities
- Learn new skills at your own pace
- Complete just-in-time training

Now that we have examined some of the ways in which virtual events are beneficial, we must consider their disadvantages so that we can provide a balanced view. Knowing the downsides to virtual events can help us to be proactive rather than reactive. We still might experience issues in the virtual environment; but by identifying those difficulties, we can put plans in place to assist us when they arise.

## The Downside to Virtual Presentations

My favorite comment often heard when someone is discussing the wonders of technology goes something like the following: *Technology is great—when it works.* No truer words were ever spoken. Technology has been a boon to many aspects of our lives. However, our dependence on technology has led us to expect it to always work. When technology fails us for whatever reason, we get frustrated.

One of my favorite professors from my doctoral program always told his students to never assume that the technology will work. His philosophy was to be prepared with a backup. Of course, in the dark ages when I attended graduate school, we did not have the types of technology that we see today; but what we did have available to us often caused problems, albeit on a much smaller scale than today's technology. Nevertheless, we persevered and overcame those little annoyances. In looking at the disadvantages or downsides to virtual presentations, however, problems with the technology can mean that the virtual event cannot take place, it ends early, or it prohibits participants from accessing it. Any type of technical difficulty in the delivery of a virtual event can result in the loss of your audience, and that is something you absolutely wish to avoid.

The following list of disadvantages is not all encompassing. We all know that when technology is involved, we can surmise that additional problems are always just one program or platform iteration away.

**Technical Difficulties**. We covered some of the concerns about technology and the difficulties inherent in the virtual environment. However, other areas of potential technical problems are outside of your purview and involve the different types of computers, tablets, and/or smartphones participants employ when accessing the virtual event. The unique operating system configurations, connection speeds, Internet browser choices, and software applications can hinder participation or deny access.

Another technical issue over which virtual presenters or facilitators have no control involves potential firewalls. If a participant is attempting to connect to your virtual presentation, webinar, or e-meeting via an employer's Internet platform, he or she may experience problems because of a corporate firewall. Again, these technical issues are not the fault of the virtual presenter or facilitator. Nevertheless, participants may become frustrated and simply disconnect from the virtual event.

Technical difficulties that virtual presenters or facilitators can control are those that arise from a lack of familiarity with the platform being used for the virtual event or the absence of support personnel to assist with the virtual event (e.g., technology person to manage the platform, person to monitor the chat area for participants' questions and comments). If you wish to deliver a successful virtual event, you want to familiarize yourself with the platform being used and to rehearse numerous times before the actual event is scheduled to take place. You also want to make sure that you have people in place to handle technology issues that may arise on your end as well as to serve as monitors for the Q&A and/or chat forum.

**Body Language Issues**. Chapter 3 in this book covers detailed information about nonverbal communication and its role in virtual events. As a disadvantage or downside, though, the inability to see the presenter or facilitator in the virtual environment as clearly (if at all) as you do in the traditional setting means that those nonverbal cues—eye contact, gestures, and facial expressions—are missing. In a traditional presentation, if a presenter pauses for effect, to build suspense, the audience knows what is occurring. In the virtual environment, if that same pause happened, participants would think the presenter lost his or her place or accidentally muted the session. Those nonverbal cues add context to a presentation and help the presenter or facilitator establish credibility with participants. When the nonverbal is missing, the presenter or facilitator must work harder to ensure participants know what is taking place at every point in the virtual event.

**Environmental Difficulties**. In traditional settings, the presenter generally controls the location, lighting, and seating. Because other individuals are in the room to hear the presentation, peer pressure keeps side conversations and disruptions to a minimum. In the virtual environment, however, the presenter or facilitator has no control over participants' environment. Participants get to choose their location for the virtual event. As such, they can be in their home, their office, or in a coffee shop. We can only imagine the distractions taking place in these environments. Also, if the presenter or facilitator mutes participants' microphones or asks them to mute their phone lines, then participants may feel free to check their e-mail, surf the Internet, or perform other tasks. No one is watching; no peer pressure is keeping those distractions out of the virtual environment. To reduce distractions and keep participants engaged, the virtual presenter or facilitator needs to build in opportunities for participation (e.g., polling, Q&A, chat). Chapters 3 and 4 provide additional information about reducing distractions in the virtual environment.

**Attendance Issues**. Many virtual events require registration. Participants are asked to complete a form designed to provide specific audience analysis information to the presenter or facilitator. While requiring registration for a virtual event does give the presenter or facilitator an idea of the number of participants who indicated they will attend, that registration does not guarantee that all of them will be present at the virtual event. Unless your virtual event is tied to a requirement for work, continuing education units, a certification or re-certification process, you may find attendance to be low. People still prefer networking in real time when they attend an event in person. If you require registration for your virtual event, you can also follow up with participants, as well as with nonparticipants, at the conclusion of your presentation or webinar. Chapter 5 in this text covers the follow-up for virtual events.

While we may find additional roadblocks or difficulties inherent in the virtual environment, the ones listed in the preceding section are the most frequently cited. Whether you are considering a virtual event or engaged in preparing for one, you want to look at both sides of the issue, the positive and negative. Be proactive in addressing potential issues while taking advantage of the opportunities presented in the virtual environment. Now that we have addressed both the advantages and disadvantages of virtual events, the following section discusses how we can use them.

## Ways We Can Use Virtual Events

Because of the opportunities virtual environments offer, we can meet across the miles in real time without having to leave the comfort of our office or home. We can invite guest speakers to deliver keynote addresses at conventions and conferences without having to pay for travel for those individuals. We can deliver sales promotions and training sessions to customers and clients from our offices—no more face-to-face cold calling required.

**Training**. Consider for a moment, the job requirements of human resource personnel prior to the advent of technology for virtual presentations. These individuals had to personally handle new employee onboarding (training for new employees); develop and deliver training for updates to employment laws, benefits, and any new or modified policies and procedures specified by the CEO and/or Board of Trustees; and schedule and participate in on-site, face-to-face interviews to hire new employees and/or promote existing employees. Now, virtual communication technologies allow for the creation and distribution of new hire training materials and just-in-time training for employees to access on demand to review specific processes and procedures. HR personnel also benefit from the ability to conduct initial interviews with job candidates without the necessity of an on-site meeting.

**Conventions and Conferences**. Convention and conference planners and directors have also benefitted from the deployment of virtual presentation technologies and platforms. The ability to secure nationally recognized guest speakers to deliver virtual presentations is one cost-saving measure convention and conference planners and directors enjoy. Paying an honorarium or speaker's fee only is far less expensive than paying that fee along with covering the guest speaker's travel (i.e., airfare, mileage) to and from the convention or conference location, hotel expenses, and meals.

In addition, convention and conferences that offer virtual sessions can attract a wider audience. While face-to-face conventions and conferences have not lost their networking appeal for most participants, the addition of a virtual component draws a more geographically dispersed audience. People who would not be able to attend an on-site event can join organizations or associations and enjoy the membership benefits of virtual conference sessions.

Another benefit of virtual presentations at conventions and conferences is that of audience participation. In a traditional presentation, audience participants must wait until the conclusion of the speech to ask questions or to contribute to a discussion. In the virtual environment, however, participants can be involved throughout the presentation. Most virtual platforms offer a space for posting questions and have tools such as hand raises, polls, and other options by which to encourage input from participants.

Unlike on-site presentations, virtual presentations have a longer shelf life. Recordings can be packaged and reused. Also, if sponsorships are involved, the sponsors receive added benefit from the continued availability of the recorded presentation.

**Education**. Educational institutions also have found uses for virtual events. Just as conventions and conferences use virtual presentations for guest speakers, so do teachers in various educational settings. They invite experts into their classrooms to speak with students on a variety of subjects. Often these guest speakers cannot physically attend the classes due to geographical location, other commitments, job responsibilities, or personal reasons; therefore, the use of a virtual platform can meet the needs of both the speaker and the class.

Furthermore, virtual platforms for mock interviews are in use at numerous colleges and universities. These platforms allow students to engage in mock interviews with a program that records the students' responses to an established set of interview questions. Professors can select questions for their mock interview assignment from a list generated by the program. Students have a set number of practice interview sessions before they must complete and record their mock interview for grading. Those recordings can be viewed by the students as often as they desire. Professors can view them and post feedback on students' performance as well.

Numerous online courses and programs require students to deliver virtual presentations as part of the courses. At the University of Nebraska, one professor requires her students to create online presentations to demonstrate their understanding of course material and how it relates to prior learning as well as to future learning and their careers. These students are demonstrating their acquisition of knowledge as part of their course requirements, but they are also familiarizing themselves with virtual platforms and the processes involved in delivering presentations in a setting outside of face-to-face or on-site.

A study of 2,587 respondents, aged 14 to 50 years, revealed several important findings related to virtual presentations (Global Research and

Insights 2018). Among respondents identified as Generation Z (defined in the study as individuals aged 14 to 23), 59 percent prefer YouTube over textbooks for learning course material. Millennials (defined in the study as encompassing individuals aged 24 to 40) indicated that textbooks have a slight edge over YouTube videos (60 percent of Millennial respondents reported a preference for textbooks); however, 55 percent of Millennial respondents indicated that YouTube was the number one preferred learning method. So, the results for the Millennial and Generation Z respondents were very close (Global Research and Insights 2018).

Nonetheless, when we consider teaching and learning, we are generally looking at Generation Z as our student population. Given that this group prefers YouTube (60 percent) and learning apps and interactive games (47 percent), you can certainly surmise that virtual presentations are likely to grow in importance in the educational setting as teachers move to craft professional virtual presentations for the platforms of choice for students.

**Meetings**. Most corporations have a global reach, with offices and employees scattered throughout the world, across datelines and time zones. Even though global expansion has been aided via technology, many of those same companies have had a worldwide presence for decades. The advent of e-meeting platforms, however, has added another element to scheduling and managing meetings. Previously, organizations had to schedule meetings at a central physical location, and attendance at these meetings by specific employees whose presence was of paramount importance led to travel costs, time away from job responsibilities, and a myriad of scheduling issues. While the use of e-meeting technology has not completely resolved the inherent scheduling dilemmas, it has provided alternatives to the requisite travel requirement as well as the ancillary expenses associated with travel.

**Webinars**. Many industries require individuals with certifications or licenses to earn continuing education units to maintain their certification or license. Webinars are one way that people can ensure they meet those requirements. Educational institutions, publishers, companies with vested interest in the fields of certification or licensure, and experts in the field offer webinars, some at low- to no-cost, to assist with professional development and re-certification needs. Individuals register for these webinars and participate in real time (synchronously) or review the recorded version (asynchronously) at a later date and time.

Some technology companies use webinars as a mechanism for introducing a new or updated version of a program to demonstrate to users the changes between the earlier version of the program and the new version or to review the basics of a newly released application. Still other organizations use webinars to promote membership in an association, including the benefits of joining.

**Sales and Support**. As mentioned in the Webinar section, companies use webinars to introduce products and updates to products, to demonstrate how a product performs, to train employees in the sale and delivery of products, and to provide support for individuals and organizations who purchase products from these organizations.

In summary, virtual events encompass webinars, e-meetings, training programs, and online presentations. These virtual events can occur in real time or via on-demand recording. They can serve as cost-saving measures for companies, offer alternative methods for product sales and service, allow individuals to make virtual presentations at conferences and conventions—or in classrooms—and enhance organizational training options. The next step is to look at the similarities and differences between face-to-face and virtual presentations. Chapter 2 will focus attention on the concepts and skills involved in delivering effective presentations in both environments.

# References

AMA Staff. 2011. "Perfect Your Virtual Presentations." http://www.ama-net.org/training/articles/perfect-your-virtual-presentations.aspx.

American Management Association. 2019. https://www.amanet.org/.

Darlin, D. June 26, 2014. "How the Future Looked in 1964: The Picturephone," *The New York Times, March of Progress*. https://www.nytimes.com/2014/06/27/upshot/how-the-future-looked-in-1964-the-picturephone.html.

Global Research and Insights. August, 2018. "Beyond Millennials: The Next Generation of Learners," Pearson. https://www.pearson.com/content/dam/one-dot-com/one-dot-com/global/Files/news/news-annoucements/2018/The-Next-Generation-of-Learners_final.pdf.

*Meetings Today.* 2013. "Virtual Event Definitions." https://www.meetingstoday.com/magazines/article-details/articleid/19191/title/virtual-event-definitions.

Novak, M. 2013. "Future Calling: Videophones in the World of the Jetsons." https://www.smithsonianmag.com/history/future-calling-videophones-in-the-world-of-the-jetsons-6789346/.

Owen, A. August 28, 2018. "The History and Evolution of the Smartphone: 1992–2018," *Text Request.* https://www.textrequest.com/blog/history-evolution-smartphone/.

Pew Research Center: Internet and Technology. February 5, 2018. "Mobile Fact Sheet." http://www.pewinternet.org/fact-sheet/mobile/.

# CHAPTER 2

# Basic Differences between Virtual Presentations and Face-to-Face Presentations

Virtual presentations and face-to-face presentations share several commonalities: an audience; a purpose; a time limit; a location; a story that has a beginning, a middle, and an ending; an expected or anticipated outcome; a plan; visuals; preparation; rehearsal; delivery; and follow-up. However, to say that they require the same skills set is not entirely true. We will examine the components of a presentation in this chapter and identify areas where the virtual presentation requires modifications to what we typically do in a traditional setting.

## Purpose

Every presentation has a purpose, no matter the platform on which it is delivered. Depending on how you are involved in the presentation, you may know the audience before you know the purpose, though. For example, you may be invited to give a presentation as part of a conference, a class, or a webinar and the invitation would tell you who—or what group—would comprise the audience. However, you still need to identify the purpose for your presentation. The purpose is the guide for all that follows in your presentation.

The purpose sets the stage for your presentation, but you also need to determine what you want it to accomplish. What do you want your audience or participants to do, to remember, or to understand at the conclusion of your presentation? A process without a goal is akin to a story with no ending.

If you are delivering instruction for a class, your goal must be tied to objectives for the lesson. A training webinar needs to have a focus on the anticipated outcome of the training—what you expect the trainees to know and/or to be able to do at the end of the training. Rarely, if ever, is a meeting called that does not have a specific purpose. Moreover, meetings use agendas to ensure their purpose is accomplished as the agenda is the guiding document for what is to be covered in a meeting.

You can easily see that all events, both virtual and traditional, have a purpose at their core. However, virtual events require an emphasis on their purpose in all promotional materials. Webinars, in particular, stand to gain a far-reaching audience if their titles accurately portray their purpose.

The next segment of this chapter discusses the expected outcomes and their importance in the planning process. Expected outcomes align with the purpose of any presentation, webinar, or meeting and are used to guide the creation and facilitation of any event.

## Expected Outcome

Both traditional face-to-face and virtual events have an expected outcome or outcomes. You may want your participants to do something (e.g., change a process or procedure, upgrade a product, try a new service), to acquire some skill or knowledge (and perhaps desire to continue learning more on the same topic), or to start a conversation about or an understanding of an idea or concept.

Whatever your expected outcome or outcomes, you must plan your presentation with that ultimate result in mind.

The next area of preparation for any presentation, webinar, or meeting is that of the audience. Regardless of the venue or platform, knowing your audience is of paramount importance, especially if you wish to achieve your projected outcome or outcomes.

## Audience

In instances where you are invited to deliver a presentation for a class, a convention or conference, or a group, you will know who the audience

is based on the location—students, members of an organization or association attending a convention or conference, or a group of people connected by religion, gender, ethnicity, or some other variable that makes
them a member of that group. Knowing your prospective audience, however, does not mean you should not conduct an analysis to gain a deeper
understanding of the demographics of the audience members.

For webinars, you have the advantage of securing audience information as part of the registration process. Webinars have a purpose, use promotional materials to market them to individuals who would benefit from
the training or knowledge development, and deploy a registration process
to collect participant information. How you design the registration form
depends on the type of information you are seeking to learn about those
individuals who sign up for your webinar. General demographic questions will provide some details to help you sketch an average audience
member profile. Using that profile, you can craft your webinar materials
to ensure that your presentation meets your audience's needs based on
their educational level, socioeconomic background, prior experience, and
any other variable you identify via your registration form.

Electronic/virtual meetings typically involve parties who know or are
known to each other. Companies use virtual meetings to serve many purposes, such as keeping employees in satellite offices connected to home
offices, assisting team members with project collaboration, and providing
a mechanism via which site managers can deliver periodic reports and
updates on projects to the CEO or board of directors. In all of these
instances, individuals involved in these virtual meetings know their audience. Therefore, audience analysis is not required to the extent needed for
other virtual events.

In planning your virtual event, however, you do have certain requirements that must be taken into consideration once your purpose and your
audience have been identified. The most important requirement is time.

## Requirements

The need to establish an appropriate time and location for your virtual
events cannot be underestimated.

## Location

As you read this statement, you may be furrowing your brow over the mention of a location for a virtual event. Location can have numerous definitions and not simply refer to a physical space, piece of land or property, office, or any other tangible location. Location can also mean the platform you choose for delivering your virtual presentation, e-meeting, webinar, or any other virtual event (e.g., Zoom, GoToMeeting, Adobe Connect). Location can also reference where you—the facilitator, presenter, meeting coordinator—are seated when accessing the selected platform for your virtual event (e.g., home, office, café or coffee shop). In addition, location can include the channel you use to access the virtual event (e.g., the mobile app, the desktop app, or the laptop app) and whether you connect via Internet service provider, Wi-Fi, or cell service provider.

You must plan for participants using a variety of locations to access your virtual event. While you, as the facilitator, have control over the location you select to create and deliver your virtual event, having some understanding of how your participants might be connecting to your virtual event can play a role in what artifacts you use or include for your presentation, webinar, or meeting. For example, when participants connect via an open or free Wi-Fi connection, those individuals may have difficulty viewing video clips or web searches in your virtual session due to the bandwidth requirements for those items. However, some of the location issues may not be relevant because of the delivery approach you choose for your virtual event, whether it is synchronous or asynchronous.

## Delivery

Based on your purpose and audience, you will also need to determine if your presentation should be delivered in real time or recorded for later viewing. Synchronous delivery means you give your presentation to participants at a set time on a specific date; your presentation is "live" and "in person." Participants can interact with the presenter or facilitator via the virtual platform—chat, polling, Q&A—during a synchronous virtual event. Moreover, if you are invited to deliver a presentation at a convention or conference, you will likely be doing so synchronously.

Asynchronous delivery means that the presenter recorded his or her presentation or webinar and that recording is then made available to any participant who registered for the event. Participants may view the recording at any time or place. The downside to an asynchronous virtual event is that participants do not have any opportunities for interaction with the presenter or facilitator. On the positive side, however, people who register for webinars or virtual presentations occasionally find themselves unable to attend the synchronous sessions, so recordings of those virtual events are helpful. Those participants can review the content even without the benefit of any interaction.

When determining the delivery setup for your virtual event, you must consider the impact of attendees' ability to participate or not participate in your virtual event. If you are conducting a training webinar, you would likely need participants' input. If you are delivering a presentation on a topic that does not lend itself to Q&A or you do not desire to entertain questions from participants, you can record your presentation and deliver it asynchronously.

When using an asynchronous approach to your virtual event, you do not have to concern yourself with the time element—for example, day of the week, time of day. However, synchronous events require a schedule. Selecting the appropriate day, date, and time can be problematic. Let's consider the time element next.

### Time

Time is another requirement for planning and delivering virtual events. You may assume I am referring to the amount of time you allot for a presentation, meeting, or webinar, and that is one of the time requirements to which I am referring. However, time also means the time of day you set as the starting point for a synchronous virtual event of any type.

As many multinational companies struggle with new employee onboarding or synchronous training sessions of any type or with scheduling e-meetings for various employee groups, they must consider the time factor. How can you schedule a synchronous e-meeting involving employees in offices that span the globe and cross numerous time and date lines? The military often faces this challenge because of troop deployment

*Table 2.1  Time zone comparison to UTC*

| GMT | DST | Military | Phonetic | Civilian Time Zones |
|---|---|---|---|---|
| +0:00 | +0:00 | Z | Zulu | UT or UTC—Universal (Coordinated) |
| +0:00 | +1:00 | | | GMT—Greenwich Mean<br>WET—Western European |
| −1:00 | +0:00 | A | Alpha | WAT—West Africa |
| −2:00 | −1:00 | B | Bravo | AT—Azores |
| −3:00 | −2:00 | C | Charlie | |
| −4:00 | −3:00 | D | Delta | AST—Atlantic Standard |
| −5:00 | −4:00 | E | Echo | EST—Eastern Standard |
| −6:00 | −5:00 | F | Foxtrot | CST—Central Standard |
| −7:00 | −6:00 | G | Golf | MST—Mountain Standard |
| −8:00 | −7:00 | H | Hotel | PST—Pacific Standard |
| −9:00 | −8:00 | J | Juliet | YST—Yukon Standard |
| −10:00 | −9:00 | K | Kilo | AHST—Alaska-Hawaii Standard<br>CAT—Central Alaska<br>HST—Hawaii Standard<br>EAST—East Australian Standard |
| −11:00 | −10:00 | L | Lima | NT—Nome |
| −12:00 | −11:00 | M | Mike | IDLW—International Date Line West |
| +1:00 | +2:00 | N | November | CET—Central European<br>FWT—French Winter<br>MET—Middle European<br>MEWT—Middle European Winter<br>SWT—Swedish Winter |
| +2:00 | +3:00 | O | Oscar | EET—Eastern European, Russia Zone 1 |
| +3:00 | +4:00 | P | Papa | BT—Baghdad, Russia Zone 2 |
| +4:00 | +5:00 | Q | Quebec | ZP4—Russia Zone 3 |
| +5:00 | +6:00 | R | Romeo | ZP5—Chesapeake Bay |
| +6:00 | +7:00 | S | Sierra | ZP6—Chesapeake Bay |
| +7:00 | +8:00 | T | Tango | WAST—West Australian Standard |
| +8:00 | +9:00 | U | Uniform | CCT—China Coast, Russia Zone 7 |
| +9:00 | +10:00 | V | Victor | JST—Japan Standard, Russia Zone 8 |
| +10:00 | +11:00 | W | Whiskey | GST—Guam Standard, Russia Zone 9 |
| +11:00 | +12:00 | X | X-ray | |
| +12:00 | +13:00 | Y | Yankee | IDLE—International Date Line East<br>NZST—New Zealand Standard<br>NZT—New Zealand |

*Source:* What does ZULU Time mean? https://www.navysite.de/what/zulu.htm.

among its various bases. Rather than determine whether to use central, eastern, mountain, or other time zone references, headquarters staff use Zulu Time (also known as Universal Time [UT] or Universal Time Coordinated [UTC]) when establishing synchronous e-meetings.

As shown in Table 2.1, Zulu Time or UTC is based on Greenwich Mean Time. UTC has no time zones and no Daylight Saving Time. Time is expressed in 24-hour increments. For example, 1:00 a.m. is expressed in UTC as zero one hundred (0100). Also, meeting dates are UTC-dependent. Therefore, if you want to schedule an e-meeting on a specific date, you would need to know the UTC for your participants so that you use the correct date for everyone involved. Plane and ship navigation use UTC as do utility radio services, shortwave listeners, and ham radio operators. The following table shows various time zones in comparison to UTC.

For most virtual events, however, you will schedule dates and times and issue invitations to attend your webinars or virtual presentations. When you are invited to deliver a virtual presentation for a convention/conference or other virtual event, you will be given a date and time for your session. In addition, if you are employed in the human resources area of your organization, you will be able to schedule virtual training sessions for new employee onboarding or product updates for sales and services at the discretion of your supervisor or you, depending on your level of responsibility.

Now that we have discussed the importance of location, delivery, and time in the development of virtual events, we must look at the role you play in that process.

# Roles

Individuals can play different roles in the creation and facilitation of virtual events. Webinars, for example, typically have two or three individuals who handle responsibilities ranging from facilitating to handling the technology to monitoring the participants' input in the chat or discussion area of the platform. If you have ever participated in a webinar, you would have been greeted by a representative of the company or organization who welcomed you to the webinar. That person introduced the presenter or facilitator and the individual managing the platform/technology for the webinar. The representative was the one who monitored the chat area for questions and then at specific periods posed those questions to the facilitator/presenter. The technology person simply remained in the background during the webinar and monitored the platform to ensure that everything ran smoothly.

These roles are very important in the virtual event process. A facilitator/presenter cannot adequately manage the platform, monitor the chat area for questions, and deliver his or her presentation, particularly if numerous participants are attending the webinar. Even if you are delivering a virtual presentation to a convention or conference audience, you still need others to assist in that process. You need someone at the convention or conference to ensure that the room setup is proper (e.g., screen, projection unit, laptop) and that the connection is working.

Often, convention centers have on-site technology companies whose coordinators provide the setup for these types of sessions. However, the convention or conference group must assign their own person to facilitate the session: to introduce the speaker, to handle the question-and-answer period during or after the presentation, and to conclude the session. In addition, if the organization has a subscription to an online meeting platform (e.g., the National Business Education Association has subscription to Adobe Connect), then the organization must have a technology person whose jobs include the creation of the URL for the virtual presentation and the monitoring of the delivery via that platform.

E-meetings may require fewer roles in their development and delivery. If the e-meeting will involve a smaller number of people, you can most likely handle the entirety of the e-meeting yourself—provided you are familiar with the platform the company uses for e-meetings and/or your company's requirements for delivering e-meetings. In some cases, organizations have an information technology department that is charged with monitoring e-meetings for technology issues. In others, managers may be able to engage in e-meetings at their discretion without the need for or interference by others.

While face-to-face presentations and meetings require individuals to assume varying roles, those roles differ from those in the virtual environment mainly because of the process itself.

Presentations at conventions and conferences may require the assistance of technology companies for the room setup, though the presentation itself is handled solely by the individual delivering it. While some associations may have a coordinator or discussant whose job is to introduce the speaker and to handle session evaluations at the conclusion, still other groups expect the speaker to introduce himself or herself and to handle question and answer in whatever manner he or she deems best or most appropriate.

The individual who calls for a meeting in the face-to-face environment is the one who prepares the agenda and leads the meeting. The meeting facilitator has no need for a technology person to be on standby for assistance but may employ the use of a secretary to take the minutes of the meeting for review and dissemination, something that also occurs in an e-meeting.

The next section of this chapter focuses on technology and how it differs between the face-to-face and virtual environments. We have addressed some of the peripheral issues involving technology previously in this section. However, we will be looking at technology more from the perspective of choices and uses in the virtual environment in the following section.

## Technology

Face-to-face and virtual presentations or events require some use of technology. In the traditional setting, presenters use some type of visual aid that usually involves a laptop, tablet, projection unit, screen, and a program (e.g., PowerPoint, Keynote, Prezi). Occasionally, presenters may access a video clip or an Internet website to display during a presentation because of its importance to the message or goal of the presentation. In those cases, presenters will use a Wi-Fi or Internet connection and speakers for sound. For traditional or on-site meetings, technology may play an ancillary role depending on the purpose of the meeting. In cases where graphics, charts, tables, or some other data analysis are required, however, technology will be integrated into the meeting plan and venue.

For virtual events, though, technology plays a major role in the creation and delivery process. We could spend a great deal of time and space discussing the available platforms, programs, and apps designed for use in delivering these virtual events. However, as we know, technology advances so rapidly that what we might discuss in this section today could well be outdated by the time this book is published—or perhaps even by the end of the next week, month, or year. Therefore, we will look at technology in its generic form with the commonalities found in most platforms, programs, and applications designed to handle the creation and delivery of virtual presentations, webinars, and meetings.

### Virtual Platform Tools

Many platforms and programs offer similar options that allow facilitators to:

- Share their desktop with participants (including programs and documents)
- Display Internet sites
- Upload and share files with participants
- Conduct polls and ask yes or no questions via specific tools designed for these purposes
- Show video clips
- Enable participants to engage in public and private chats and to post questions for the presenter to answer at some designated point during the session
- Allow participants to use their webcams for specific purposes (e.g., introductions)
- Mute participants' microphones when needed (to stop feedback or to manage input if number of participants is large)

Specific platforms even offer participants an opportunity to collaborate via meeting rooms.

Facilitators of virtual events must determine how best to use technology tools as part of their presentation, webinar, or meeting. The choice of tools should follow the purpose of the virtual event.

You do not wish to overwhelm your participants with too many tools or choices if they are unnecessary to achieving your goal.

The following list of tools is not all encompassing but includes those most likely to be available on virtual event platforms.

A) Audio
B) PowerPoint and document sharing
C) Application and desktop sharing
D) Whiteboards
E) Chat
F) Polling
G) Annotation tools
H) Recording
I) Webcams and video

Regardless of availability, however, you must choose your tools with participants in mind as well. While the use of a video clip may seem a good idea when planning your virtual event, participants who are using public Wi-Fi or their cell service provider or who have slow or spotty Internet connection speeds may be unable to access the video or to view it in real time. Videos require a great deal of bandwidth and can be problematic no matter how good the intentions of the facilitator are as to the purpose for including it.

Virtual presentations and webinars fare much better when the facilitator or presenter includes polls and question-and-answer opportunities within the actual presentation or webinar.

Participants tend to engage in other activities while watching a presentation or participating in a webinar, particularly if their attention wanders due to the lecture style of the presenter or facilitator. You want to periodically ask questions that can be answered using one of the platform tools (e.g., the thumbs-up or thumbs-down icon, the raised hand icon) and to allow time for questions posed by the participants in the chat area of the platform.

One of the missing pieces of virtual events comes from the absence of nonverbal feedback from your audience. In face-to-face presentations, you can see your audience members' faces and determine if your information is making sense or if you need to change up your process and to ask questions or seek input from the group. In a virtual environment, you do not have that feedback on which to draw, so you must simply build in those polling and Q&A opportunities to ensure that participants' attention spans are not exceeded by your presentation.

One of the most important caveats regarding technology tools for virtual events has to do with familiarity with the platform. If you are going to use a specific application or program, you should know how to use it properly, including all the tools the platform has available. Nothing is more troubling for participants than to see that the presenter or facilitator is inexperienced in using the platform. You need to be able to create the meeting, presentation, or webinar location and to share that URL with participants in an invitation to attend. You also must know what steps the participants will need to take to be able to access the meeting, presentation, or webinar.

Some programs require participants to download a program to access the virtual meeting or event via the URL provided. Even though Adobe Flash has largely been replaced with HTML5 for video viewing, at least one virtual meeting or webinar program still requires it. Therefore, if you choose to use that program, you will need to advise your participants that they must use a device on which Adobe Flash can operate and that they must have it downloaded and running on their computer or laptop prior to attempting to access the meeting or webinar URL. Having this information available for your participants is vital to the success of your virtual events.

Also, you want to encourage your participants to access the program you will be using and to deploy the setup wizard for audio and video components. Having participants handle these duties prior to the day of or time of the virtual event ensures that the event will begin on time without any interruptions or questions regarding access. We usually call these housekeeping concerns because they help facilitators and presenters clean up any potential problem spots before the actual virtual event begins.

Additional discussion regarding practice and rehearsal appears later in this chapter where you will be reminded of the need to be proficient with your use of any program or application you use in the virtual environment. As previously discussed, if you are fortunate enough to have a technology support person assigned to your webinars or presentations, you have some breathing room regarding unforeseen technology incidents that may arise. However, the presence of a technology support person does not negate your responsibility as the presenter or facilitator to know how to properly use the platform, program, or application.

Now that we have looked at the technology side of presentations, we next contemplate the plan. The plan for your presentation, webinar, or meeting (both virtual and traditional) is your roadmap to expected outcomes or what you expect of your audience or participants.

## Plan

For both virtual and traditional presentations, you must have a plan established to get you from point A to point B—from beginning to end. In the preceding section, I mentioned that the plan is something akin to a roadmap that guides you to your expected outcomes. Virtual presentations, webinars, and meetings require a more detailed plan because of the technology involved. Webinars also need extensive planning if you are offering them via invitation and requiring interested parties to register for them. The invitation and registration steps mean you need a marketing plan as well to ensure your webinar is promoted across proper channels and targets the people who would be most interested in your topic.

When planning your traditional presentation content, you typically create an outline of the information you wish to share, determine how you wish to begin your presentation (e.g., ask a question, give a quote, provide statistics), decide on the three to four major points you wish you cover in your presentation, and determine what type of visual aids you wish to use to complement your presentation. Your plan centers around the time allotted to you for your presentation and the results of the audience analysis you conducted to better understand what your participants want to learn. Your goal is to create a presentation that meets the needs of your audience and to craft ancillary materials (e.g., visuals, handouts) that complement your information.

Virtual presentations require the same steps but also add the technology choice (e.g., platform, venue) and the processes required to get your presentation materials into the proper form for delivery via your chosen platform, program, or application. For example, if you plan to use a PowerPoint slideshow during your virtual event, you want to get that file uploaded to your platform before the event is set to begin. If you plan to use your PowerPoint file as a handout for participants, you want to put it in the proper form and have it set to "push out" to participants either at the start of or the day before the virtual event. You would do the same with any handouts you desire to share.

The sharing of information requires you to be prepared well in advance of the virtual presentation or webinar. Unlike traditional settings, you cannot wait until the last minute to add something to your presentation—whether it be adding text to a PowerPoint slide or adding slides to a PowerPoint slideshow—you do not have the luxury of delaying in a virtual environment. You can see why the plan for your virtual event is paramount in its importance.

From planning to preparing, you are working to ensure that your participants have the experience they desire and that you achieve the outcome you planned for from the beginning. As with any presentation, preparation is key to success.

## Preparation

Presentations of any type require preparation. If you are invited to deliver a virtual presentation for a convention or conference, you are considered the expert. You want to establish credibility as that expert. Therefore, you cannot "wing it" and hope that everything works out. Outlining your topic, drafting speech notes, creating ancillary materials—all of those are part of your preparation. If you were delivering a traditional presentation, you would want to familiarize yourself with the room layout, where the podium (what type of podium) is located, how the sound system works, if you need a microphone, among other important factors. The virtual environment requires similar preparation. You need to identify the type of virtual platform being used, familiarize yourself with the tools available via that platform and the platform's operation, and familiarize yourself with the audio and video systems (e.g., do you need to use a headset and microphone), among others.

As part of your preparation procedures, you will also create any visuals you plan to use (e.g., PowerPoint slideshow). You may wish to use websites to display important information or video clips to participants. If so, you must identify those and secure the proper URLs for them. Perhaps you want to share your desktop—a specific application such as Microsoft Word—to demonstrate a procedure or process. If so, you need to prepare for that as well.

In the end, your credibility as a presenter is impacted by your ability to seamlessly deliver your virtual presentation. If you have technical issues or if something in your visuals does not work properly, your credibility falters. How can you ensure that everything flows smoothly? Practice, practice, practice.

## Practice/Rehearsal

As mentioned previously, your credibility as a speaker can be impacted by many factors. Knowing your information is the first concern. You are an expert, so you want to demonstrate your expertise. Do not read to your participants. Talk to them using a conversational tone. Develop effective visuals following the proper rules for design of PowerPoint slides. Ensure that you have the correct links for any websites or programs you wish to display during your virtual event. Know your platform. What tools do you have at your disposal? Which ones do you plan to use? Do you plan to take questions from participants? If so, when?

Once you have answered these questions (usually as part of your plan and preparation), you are ready to begin rehearsing the delivery of your presentation. Yes, even virtual presentations require practice. If you do not know what platform is being used for your virtual event, check with the planners of the conference or convention to obtain the answer to that question. Ask for early access for practice sessions. If your organization has a subscription to the platform, schedule practice times. The goal is to practice using the platform that will be in use for the virtual event. The more familiar you are with the platform, the better. However, familiarity with the tools you will be using for the virtual event does not negate the need for rehearsal of what you plan to say. As always, practice allows us to identify our strengths and our weaknesses and gives us ample opportunity to improve.

## Delivering the Virtual Event

You have followed the required steps in the virtual event process and are now ready to deliver the presentation or webinar or to facilitate the e-meeting. Have faith in your abilities, your knowledge and skills, and know that butterflies are always a sign that you want to do the best job possible for the participants. You want to give them what they signed up for—and more. Be confident in your preparation. Sign on to the virtual event platform a few minutes early and speak with those early participants who like to explore the virtual platform (see Appendix 1, Virtual Event Checklist). Taking those few minutes to familiarize yourself with some of the people who are attending your virtual event allows you to get comfortable, to warm up. If you were delivering your presentation in person, you would do the same thing. You would speak to people as they arrived; you would introduce yourself and ask them what brought them to the session. If you do this in the virtual environment, you will find that by the time the actual event begins, you are calm and those butterflies are settled in.

Once you complete your virtual event, you have a few activities that you want to handle. The next section discusses the need for follow-up at the conclusion of a virtual event and how best to handle those responsibilities. A presenter's job does not end just because the virtual presentation is complete. You still have a few things you should do to ensure participants had the experience you planned for them.

## Follow-Up

Virtual presentations just like some traditional ones require a follow-up or evaluation. Most conventions and conferences ask attendees to complete session evaluations to help presenters learn how well their presentation was received. In the virtual environment, those evaluations take on a higher level of importance. Participants in virtual events need to be asked to evaluate the session as soon as possible after the session ends. The best opportunity occurs right before the presenter closes the event. At that point, participants can be asked to click on a link and complete a session evaluation. You generally have a higher level of participation with that type of request than you would with sending a *thank you for attending* e-mail with a link to an evaluation form embedded therein.

In addition, presenters and facilitators of virtual events—especially webinars—may wish to follow up with participants via e-mail. The participants who attended the session will appreciate the thank you, and participants who registered but were unable to attend will also appreciate a *we missed you*-type e-mail message with a link to the webinar or virtual presentation recording.

The power of "thank you" should never be underestimated, especially in the world of virtual events. People remember the kindness and generosity of the presenter and are more likely to return to that individual for additional training or knowledge acquisition needs. Those registered participants who were unable to attend the virtual session will also remember the presenter who took the time to say they were missed and who provided a link to a recording of the event. Follow-up is vital to success for virtual events, and you should embrace that responsibility.

Now that we have explored some of the basic differences between traditional and virtual presentations, we must move forward with establishing some basic guidelines for delivering and facilitating virtual events. Chapter 3 looks at the nonverbal communication components that play an important role in becoming a successful virtual presenter.

# CHAPTER 3

# Developing and Delivering Virtual Presentations: The Nonverbal Aspect

Based on the proliferation of virtual events and the absence of instructional materials on the topic, we need to establish some basic guidelines that will make us more effective virtual presenters and e-meeting and webinar facilitators. If you train others in how to create and deliver presentations, you will need to include instruction on the impact of the virtual environment and the changes necessary to be effective in that venue.

Do not assume that if an individual knows and can demonstrate the skills for creating and delivering effective presentations in the traditional setting, that the same person will perform as well in the virtual environment. A great example is that of the college professor whose on-campus classes have waiting lists for enrollment because of the professor's teaching style, use of stories to convey personal meaning to the course content, and infusion of humor to create a comfortable learning environment who then attempts to create an online version of the same course. The professor assumes that he can simply take the same materials and put them into the online learning management system, create and upload some video lectures using the same stories and humor, and add a few discussion requirements, tests, and quizzes. Students will want to take the online version of the class. Not so fast, professor.

In the traditional classroom, the professor has the students in the class with whom to engage. If he uses a humorous quip—or one he believes is humorous—the response of students in the class lets him know if the joke landed in the way he intended or if it fell flat. He also can infuse a great deal of nonverbal communication via his vocalics and body language to help deliver the message in the proper form. He has a captive audience, one sitting directly in front of him. He can see facial expressions—eye rolls, smiles, frustration, aggravation—in real time. If students display quizzical expressions or look at their smartphones during discussions, the professor can quickly change his message. He can ask questions to ascertain understanding of the material to see if he needs to give further explanation. He can give a quiz to help him ascertain the students' level of knowledge, thus assisting with moving to other material to avoid boredom. The professor can adapt his message on the spot based on students' nonverbal feedback. His traditional classroom is a synchronous setting. Everything happens in real time.

The virtual environment does not provide the same opportunities for "on the fly" changes to our presentations, lectures, discussions, or meetings. We must take additional steps to prepare before the actual event. Also, we rarely see our participants in virtual presentations and webinars. Issues with bandwidth and the number of participants in any of those sessions prevent us from being able to turn on our webcams and leave them on for the duration of the event. Even if you could see each participant in your virtual event, the nonverbal signals would be limited to facial expressions only so you would not see fidgeting, multitasking, or other examples of inattention, disinterest, or disagreement.

So, being a virtual presenter or facilitator requires some specialized training to overcome the challenges posed by the virtual environment. Chapters 1 and 2 introduced the concepts, and the remainder of this chapter provides specific training suggestions to prepare for your virtual event.

When preparing for a virtual presentation, webinar, or e-meeting, you need to consider several areas: your appearance, your presentation style, your use of nonverbal communication, and your proficiency with operating the technology.

In addition, you have to ensure accessibility. Is your virtual event and any materials associated with it accessible to any participant desiring to attend? The following checklists and explanations should assist with your preparation for and delivery of virtual events. While I have tried to include as many factors as possible, you may find as you become more proficient in delivering presentations, webinars, and e-meetings that additional concerns arise for which you were unprepared. Make note of those incidences and share your experiences with this author, with your colleagues, and with others who are engaged in training people to deliver effective virtual events. Explain how you addressed those issues. If we truly wish to compile a best practices compendium for delivering effective virtual events, we all must share personal stories of success, failure, and learning. As I noted in Chapter 3, very little research exists about the teaching of virtual presentation skills. We need to change that dynamic.

## What Effective Virtual Presenters Need to Know

Individuals who give speeches, make presentations, facilitate meetings, and deliver training have developed those skills needed to be effective in their respective roles. However, as mentioned previously in this book, simply being an experienced presenter, speaker, trainer, or facilitator does not translate to being effective in the virtual environment. We will begin our discussion with the visible portion of virtual presentation—your appearance.

### You Only Get One Chance to Make a Good First Impression

As a young student, I remember my teachers stressing that we should always dress professionally whenever we were going to give a speech in class, go on an interview, or participate in any organizational competition. We learned that professional dress referred to a suit. In my current college classes, I still cover this topic and remind students that you cannot recreate a first impression. When someone meets you for the first time, your image is the first thing noted. We also discuss how dressing professionally for a speech versus wearing the usual jeans and tee-shirt/sweatshirt impacts the person's performance. We recognize—even subconsciously—that we are engaged in something that requires a higher level of performance when we are dressed professionally. Therefore, students who wear professional attire for a class presentation are the ones who typically score higher grades on that assignment.

Dressing for a virtual presentation differs from that of a face-to-face speech. In most cases, the online platform being used allows participants to view only the upper portion of the speaker's or facilitator's body—the head, neck, and shoulder areas. Some platforms, especially those designed for meetings and online interviews, allow for more visibility. In those cases, you can see the upper half of the speaker or facilitator, as well as anything directly behind and around the speaker.

So, before you decide what you will wear and what location you will use for your virtual event, you need to know what platform you will be using. The platform determines the visibility of your environment and you. If you are unsure of the platform and/or the capability of that platform regarding visibility of the presenter or facilitator, err on the side of caution and use the following guidelines to prepare.

- **Dress:** Wear professional attire. Select a solid color, as any herringbone, striped, or plaid material may result in distortion. If you wear a suit jacket, select a dress shirt in a neutral color that complements the color of the suit jacket. Avoid wearing white as it can also create problems with video distortion. Generally, women should wear a blouse with a high neckline, and male presenters who wear a suit should include a tie as part of their attire. The best color choices for blouses are cool blues, purples, pastels, and natural hues. If possible, you should find out the color of the background for your virtual presentation so you can make sure to choose a color for your suit and accessories that will not clash with it.

- **Grooming:** Make sure your hair is not limiting visibility. You want to make eye contact with your participants (yes, even though they are virtual) and do not want your hair/bangs to encroach on your face or to cover your eyes. Male presenters should attempt to ensure that any facial hair is not distracting and does not obscure the mouth. Participants with a hearing impairment may like to read lips, and if your facial hair (e.g., mustache and/or beard) prevents them from being able to see your lips, you can be limiting their accessibility. Female presenters should select make-up options carefully. Some lipstick colors can give the appearance of bleeding onto the teeth, so the best option is to choose neutral shades rather than bright, bold colors. Also, all presenters should endeavor to limit earrings to those that fit close to the ear—no hoops or dangling earrings or facial rings. Your goal is to avoid anything that might distract from your presentation. Because you are using a virtual platform that limits how much of the presenter or facilitator is visible, you need to recognize that anything—no matter how small you may deem it to be—can create a diversion by causing participants to fixate on that item or area.

- **Location:** Select a location that provides the proper atmosphere for your virtual event. You do not want to be in a heavily trafficked location or one with lots of noise. You also want to ensure that anything on display directly behind or around you is not distracting. Using a conference room with a blank wall for a backdrop can be a good choice. If you choose to use your office, make sure that any photos, artwork, or other items are moved out of view. Participants tend to focus on things behind you and attempt to discern what they are, who is in the photo, what your certificate says, and so on. Make sure the lighting in the room you select is appropriate. You do not want the light to be too bright and wash you out, but you also do not want the room to be too dark and create problems with visibility. Determining the proper lighting will require you to practice with your web camera. Record a practice video of you in the space where you wish to present or facilitate your virtual event. View it and determine if the lighting is proper. Again, poor lighting affects the entire quality of your virtual event.

- **Sound:** As mentioned in the previous bullet point, you want to use the proper location for your virtual event. You want the noise to be at a minimal level. You cannot facilitate or present your virtual event in a library, computer lab, dormitory room, apartment, home, or any location with excessive noise and the inability to control the noise levels. If you have pets, you would not want to hold your virtual event in your home or apartment because your pets may begin barking and create a major distraction. Also, having a significant other, a roommate or roommates that may arrive home at any point can also be problematic. Find a location where you have control over the noise. If need be, place a note on your door that explains to anyone who may approach that you are involved in a virtual event and would appreciate not being disturbed—or ask them not to knock if you think that would be a better approach. The goal is to keep any noise to a minimum to avoid distractions. Any unexpected noise can startle you and cause you to lose track of where you are in your presentation and can result in participants being unable to hear you as well. Check construction details or deadlines for any location you are considering. You do not want to find yourself in a location you believed would be perfect only to find that remodeling is taking place with lots of hammering occurring on the very date and time you planned your virtual event to take place.

Dress, grooming, sound, and location are all very important to creating that best first impression of your virtual event—and you as the presenter or facilitator. These areas are also important to the establishment of credibility of the presenter or facilitator.

While most people believe credibility hinges on the factual nature of the information being shared by the presenter or facilitator in any virtual event, the presenter's or facilitator's ability to dress appropriately and to manage the platform and all the areas involved in the virtual event carry equal and sometimes greater weight in the overall success of that event.

### Think and Act Like a Radio or Television Newscaster

In Chapter 1, we considered that television newscasters are like virtual presenters. They continually deliver news and information in a virtual environment without the benefit of being able to see their audience or to interact with them. Virtual presenters and facilitators can learn a great deal from those successful newscasters, however.

- Newscasts use blocks or segments for organization. Each block or segment covers a specific topic. These segments do not have uniform time or length requirements. Instead, the length of a segment depends on the topic, its importance, and the amount of time required to tell the full story. Understandably, segments in a newscast are organized in order of interest to the audience. The more interesting the story, the higher the placement in the order of segments. In the world of virtual presentations, you should consider the following when planning your event.

- Topics I must cover during the presentation or e-meeting
- Placement of segments starting with most interesting one
- Depth of each topic
- Time allotted to discussion or Q&A

- Newscasts make efficient use of time. You do not see newscasters panic. They know how much time they have available to cover their topics, and they do not try to add more information than can easily fit into that time segment. In other words, they do not attempt to "wing it." Also, newscasters know that time is too precious to waste on added words or vocal nonfluencies (e.g., uh, ah, um). Virtual presenters should make efficient use of their time to cover only the information that will fit into their allotted segment. Following the examples of newscasters, they should also avoid the use of any vocal nonfluencies.

- In Chapter 2, we read about the roles of individuals in the virtual presentation, webinar, and e-meeting environments. In the world of newscasting, you also see individual roles such as anchor, weather caster, producer, and so on. As previously discussed, virtual events function more effectively when the presenter has assistance from others. For example, having a technology person to handle the platform and its myriad of responsibilities means that the presenter or facilitator does not have to be concerned with any technical issue. Just like the producer of the newscaster, the technology person for virtual events makes sure the program is working effectively, monitors the chat forum, oversees the Q&A function, and handles many other production-related activities. So, presenters and facilitators need to assign roles to individuals to ensure that the organization and delivery of their presentation, webinar, or e-meeting is seamless.

- Newscasters also use transitions exceedingly well to move from one segment or topic to the next. Presenters can emulate that behavior by using simple hand-offs such as "now that we have talked about topic a, let's move on to our next area, topic b." Avoid jumping from topic to topic without transitioning. People need those verbal signposts to be able to follow you. Without them, you have lost your participants. Just a quick note as well, you should not rely solely on a visual to signal transition. Visuals serve to complement your presentation, not take the place of your words. Therefore, even in cases where you use visuals tied to your transition from one topic to another, you still need to verbally confirm that you are transitioning. Think about the newscast scenario and how pictures and images appear in time with the transitional words of the anchor or weathercaster. If the producer simply "threw an image or photo" onto the screen, the viewers would be confused and likely would complain or simply change the channel to another program.

- Newscasts use tools to gain an audience's attention and to maintain their audience's attention. The list of these aids can be rather lengthy and not totally comprehensive: videos, photos, slides, live or recorded talent, graphics, whiteboards, green screen technology, interviews, sounds, sound bites, music, backgrounds, staging, and voice. Further discussion about the voice as a tool can be found in the nonverbal section that follows. In summary, remember when choosing the tools for your virtual event to consider which ones would be most effective—which ones will add meaning to the presentation, webinar, or e-meeting. You want the ones that will create the greatest impact. You always want to consider your audience's needs and how the use of some tools might impact their ability to participate in your virtual event, or even to adequately access the event depending on their Internet connection.

Newscasts can certainly provide ideas to ensure your virtual events are successful. Also, reviewing the performance of your favorite newscaster or radio announcer can prove useful and help you identify specific tips or tricks you want to adopt for your virtual events.

### Nonverbal Communication Is Not Just for Traditional Settings

People tend to think of nonverbal communication as being something useful in the traditional settings. Of course, Mehrabian's work was misconstrued but resulted in everyone believing that in a face-to-face set-ting, what people say through body language is more important than the words they utter (nonverbal accounts for 93 percent of the meaning of conversation in a face-to-face setting). Regardless of the veracity of the 93 percent doctrine credited to Mehrabian, nonverbal communication is an important aspect in *any* communication setting.

Rather than spend pages discussing nonverbal communication—what it is, its functions, and the types of nonverbal communication—we will focus on the role it plays in the development of a dynamic, professional on-screen presence. The types of nonverbal communication involved in this process include kinesics (body language), paralanguage (the voice), and proxemics (dress). We have previously covered the importance of dress in a virtual setting and will now consider the importance of body language.

**Kinesics**. Kinesics refers to the study of communication via body language.

For presenters, body language can play an important role in establish-ing a relationship with the participants in a virtual event.

Most virtual events involve the presenter or facilitator being seated during the session. Therefore, the following techniques will focus on ways to become a more effective presenter when seated.

### Look Relaxed and Confident

You do not want to appear to be a *talking head*, something very hard to avoid in a virtual setting. You want to be relaxed and appear as if you are talking one-on-one in a real-time setting. Avoid leaning back in your chair or leaning so far forward that your head and face fill the entire space on camera. Your goal should be to assume a position that allows you to use your hands to emphasize points during your presentation, webinar, or e-meeting. Use the following guidelines to assist you.

- Rest your hands on the table in front of you with most of your forearms on the table.

- Keep your elbows off the table to prevent yourself leaning on them and making your shoulders appear hunched.

While certain hand movements can serve to emphasize specific points in your presentation, you want to avoid excessive movement. Hand movements appear more pronounced on the screen than in person because you are framed in a limited space. If you move your hands frequently in and out of the space, your movements can be distracting to participants. You also want to refrain from getting your hands too close to the camera. The closer your hands are to the camera, the larger they appear—especially in relation to your image.

By keeping your forearms on the table in front of you and keeping your hands separated, you reduce the tendency to fidget—another distracting behavior that you want to avoid in a virtual event. Participants tend to focus on whatever is happening on the screen, even when distracting, so you want to avoid giving them something to focus on that takes their attention away from what you are discussing.

So, you may be wondering at this point exactly when you can use your hands to emphasize something in your presentation. You have numerous opportunities to use your hand gestures; they just need to occur at the right time and for specific purposes.

- When discussing small numbers
- When indicating increases or decreases in something
- When giving instructions or directions
- When showing comparisons

Obviously, this short list does not include every occasion when you might use your hands in an effective way to emphasize a point in your virtual presentation. Nonetheless, you want to ensure that when you do use your hands that you are using them to complement your presentation and not detract from it.

I advise my students when preparing for a face-to-face presentation to take two books of approximately equal weight, hold one book in each hand, and stand in front of a mirror. Then, practice their speech. If they move their hands while speaking, those gestures are natural and part of their normal speaking process. If their hands do not move from their sides, I advise them that they should not attempt to add hand gestures during their presentations as they will appear stiff and the movements will appear unnatural.

Virtual platforms provide you the option of recording your presentations—including your practice attempts. Use that tool and record a full run through of your virtual presentation, webinar, or e-meeting. Watch your posture and gestures. Do you look comfortable and confident? Are you using your hands to complement or emphasize? Or, are your fidgeting? Slumping in your chair? Remember that your nonverbal behavior conveys your credibility to your participants. Rehearse until you can see that your appearance conveys confidence but, more importantly, until you feel confident in your abilities to use the technology and to properly communicate using body language and gestures.

Another area of nonverbal communication in the realm of kinesics or body language is affect displays. The most visible part of the presenter or facilitator in the virtual environment is the face; therefore, affect displays play a vital communication role there.

**Affect Displays.** Affect displays are facial movements that complement the verbal message. Anything that shows the emotional condition of the speaker—smiles, nods, or frowns—are considered affect displays. As a virtual presenter or facilitator, you can use your facial movements to show the participants how you feel about what you are discussing, to engage them with the material, or to encourage them to participate.

**Eye Contact.** A famous expression, *the eyes are the windows to the soul,* has limited applicability in the virtual environment, especially for the presenter or facilitator who cannot see the participants. However, being unable to directly connect with your participants via eye contact does not mean that eye contact is not important in virtual events. One of the most difficult parts of delivering or facilitating a virtual presentation, webinar, or e-meeting is where to look while speaking. In a traditional setting, you have a live audience sitting in front of you with whom to connect, to make eye contact. In the virtual world, though, you have a computer screen and a web camera.

One of the biggest issues I see in my students' virtual presentations is that they look at the computer screen rather than the webcam. Some of that behavior is born out of experience with using computers and always looking at the screen when keying a report or searching the Internet for information. And, of course, some of the issue stems from lack of experience in delivering virtual presentations. Delivering a virtual event can be likened to a cumulative skill such as playing tennis or keyboarding. If you learn how to play tennis on your own without instruction, you typically learn incorrect form and procedure. The same is true of keyboarding. If you never take a keyboarding class to learn proper finger placement, you learn the hunt-and-peck method and are always at a disadvantage when attempting to key a lengthy document or to quickly respond to questions in a setting requiring use of the keyboard.

Delivering virtual presentations is no different. If you do not learn the proper way to sit, what nonverbal gestures are appropriate, and where to look when presenting, you adopt whatever approach is easiest without thought to proper form. The more you engage in the virtual environment, the more you repeat these same processes until they become engrained and become habits—even though they are bad habits. Attempting to unlearn an improper behavior is more difficult than simply learning the proper procedure at the outset.

The goal of a virtual presenter or facilitator is to connect with the participants. The best way to make that connection is through eye contact. Therefore, virtual presenters and facilitators need to know that for purposes of a virtual event, the web camera is the audience or participants.

Teaching yourself to visualize the camera as people is difficult; however, if you train yourself to look beyond the camera and to see the actual participants in your virtual event (in your mind's eye), you can begin to build that positive habit of making eye contact in the proper way.

We all know that presenters in traditional settings do not stare at the audience the entire length of the presentation. They move their eyes from person to person, look at their notes, or glance at the screen or to the side. So, virtual presenters would not be expected to stare at the web camera for the duration of the virtual event either. One of the tricks I use to ensure I make eye contact with my virtual audience is to post a sticky note or some other type of note above the web camera that says "LOOK AT YOUR

AUDIENCE!" so I remember where to focus my eyes. Even after much practice, unlearning the screen behavior is almost impossible. Therefore, the more reminders I give myself, the better.

Eye contact is important, even in the virtual environment so we want to ensure that we do not neglect that aspect of presenting and facilitating. However, we also need to position ourselves so that we are not seated too close to our web camera because the closer you sit, the more pronounced your facial and eye movements become. Remember the instructions from the section on posture and hand gestures above where we were reminded of how to position ourselves in front of the computer and web camera. The same can be said for eye contact. One rule of thumb is to ensure that your camera is positioned so that the image includes the view from the top of your head down to the desk in front of you. You do not want your eye movements to become too exaggerated and this web camera placement ensures that will not happen.

The next area of nonverbal communication involves the voice. One of the tools mentioned in the newscaster's area of this chapter was the voice. Most of us likely accept the idea that the voice could be considered a tool, but do we know how best to use our voice in a virtual event? Therefore, we need some explanation as to best practices for using our voice as a tool.

**Paralanguage**. Paralanguage is the nonverbal category encompassing the voice. It refers to how something is said, rather than what words are said. Have you ever said or heard someone say "It wasn't what he said; it was how he said it?" If so, you have some understanding of paralanguage and how it is useful in our interactions, specifically in presentations. Paralanguage has been divided into the following four categories.

- **Voice qualities:** Voice qualities refer to the voice itself and include such things as pitch, rhythm, tempo, and volume. Voice qualities can make a great deal of difference in the interpretation of a verbal message.
- **Vocal characterizers:** Vocal characterizers include such vocalizations as clearing the throat, coughing, yawning, laughing, grunting, and crying. Characterizers are distracting and annoying.
- **Vocal qualifiers:** Vocal qualifiers refer to variations in tone or intensity of speech.

- **Vocal segregates:** Vocal segregates are simply pauses—period of silence between words—but may include ahs, ums, and other nonfluencies.

While we want to avoid vocal characterizers and vocal segregates as much as possible, we do need to focus on our pitch, rhythm, tempo, volume, and variations in our tone or intensity of our speech when delivering or facilitating virtual events. I have had the unfortunate experience of being in a presentation delivered by someone who could not refrain from clearing his throat. It happened so frequently that most everyone in the room wanted to offer the speaker a glass of water or to ask if he would like to reschedule the session. I also have listened to enough student presentations that included so many vocal segregates that I started to use a system for counting the number of times I heard "ah," "um," or "you know" in the course of the 5-minute speech. For many students, hearing that they used those vocal segregates as many as 60 to 100 times in a 5-minute presentation was eye opening. Even those who used them 25 to 30 times were stunned at the frequency of occurrence. I certainly could blame the situation on lack of preparation or failure to practice. However, some of the issue stems from students' inability to recognize their tendency to use the vocal segregates in the place of silence as a crutch based on prior learning that silence in a presentation meant they had lost their place or were not prepared for their speech. Silence to them was not golden but representative of a grade for poor performance.

One of my favorite scenes demonstrating the importance of paralanguage occurs in a movie, *Ferris Bueller's Day Off*. His teacher is calling the roll in class and repeatedly says *Bueller, Bueller, Bueller* and all in the same monotone voice. I cannot imagine listening to this individual teach a class or deliver a presentation. We all have attended classes or presentations facilitated by individuals whose lack of paralanguage skills has left us reeling, either from boredom or frustration. If this occurs in the virtual environment, you lose your participants to other things: e-mail, surfing the web, or reading articles or books. You cannot see them; therefore, they feel a sense of freedom to do whatever appeals to them. If you cannot hold their attention or involve them in your presentation, webinar, or e-meeting, you can rest assured they have no problem with completing other tasks.

The online environment provides enough opportunities for you to lose your audience's attention, so you don't want to help them by falling into a trap of your own making—the monotone, soft-spoken, mumbling rambler. As much as you may dislike hearing your own recorded voice, you must take the opportunity to record your presentation practices and to review them for language quality. You want to check for the following in your vocalics.

- A dynamic range of voice (changes in tone and pitch)
- Enthusiasm (being animated in your delivery)
- Moderate sound (neither too soft nor too loud but able to be clearly heard and understood)
- Articulateness (put endings on your words and pronounce them correctly)
- Vocal nonfluencies (ah, um, er, you know—and frequency of occurrence)

You should feel free to emphasize important facts or information and to repeat where necessary. You want to ensure your participants get the main points of your presentation, webinar, or e-meeting and that may require adding emphasis to specific points of information—repetition is one of the best ways to do so. Use Appendix 2, Self-Evaluation Form for Virtual Presentations, as part of your review. You can mark those functions you performed well and add comments for improvement where needed.

You can use nonverbal communication to your advantage in your virtual presentations, webinars, and e-meetings. However, you must understand the purpose these elements serve and how to make them work for you. The virtual environment adds a different set of challenges but nothing that a well-trained presenter or facilitator cannot overcome. By following the guidelines in this chapter, you will be well on your way to becoming an effective, sought-after presenter or facilitator in the virtual environment.

# CHAPTER 4

# Developing and Delivering Virtual Presentations: Accessibility and Accommodation

Planning for a virtual event encompasses many areas of responsibility, not the least of which is ensuring that your presentation, webinar, or e-meeting is accessible to participants. The following guidelines can assist you in designing your virtual event to meet participants' accessibility or accommodation needs.

- Send out your invitation to your presentation, webinar, or e-meeting with a link to the registration form (registration form must include a question about accommodations). You can tell your invitees what platform is being used for the virtual event and ask them to let you know if they need any type of accommodation such as live captions and/or digital or text versions of the materials.
- If you use a virtual event announcement without a registration requirement, you must assume that you will have some participants who need accommodations especially since approximately 10 percent of the general public has some type of disability. If you do not wish to conduct some type of registration to identify the accommodations needed by your participants, then you must provide them anyway. At a minimum, you need to set up live captioning. You will also want to include a note in your event announcement that captioning will be provided. At present, only one virtual platform offers real-time captioning. Others are working to add that

option. Therefore, you must secure live captioning via an outside vendor.

- Send any materials to caption provider. These materials are helpful to the caption provider as they provide proper spellings of names, explanation for acronyms, and specific event language so that the captions can be as accurate as possible.

Now that you have the live caption portion of your virtual event handled, you will move to the visuals that will be part of your presentation, webinar, or e-meeting.

Visuals are an important component of virtual presentations, webinars, or e-meetings. As mentioned previously, participants' attention can wander quite easily in the virtual environment, but visuals can help maintain their attention, especially well-designed, supportive visuals. In addition to ensuring that the visuals complement the presentation, however, you also must consider issues of accessibility and accommodation in their design.

You have numerous choices for visuals to accompany your virtual event. You can use PowerPoint slideshows, websites, or video clips. You can share your desktop and showcase documents, charts, tables, graphs, or photos. Most often, though, you will create a slideshow to share with your participants as the creation of that visual does not require access to an Internet site. As mentioned previously in this book, if the virtual presenter or facilitator requires participants to view video clips or to navigate to websites that require large amounts of bandwidth, participants using free Wi-Fi or their smartphones as hot spots for accessing the Internet can experience slow livestreaming or the inability to connect. Therefore, PowerPoint slideshows tend to be the most often used visual for virtual events, whether presentation, webinar, or e-meeting.

Despite being the most frequently used tool for virtual events, most PowerPoint slides are ineffective. Most often, authors of these slides are unaware of the tools provided in PowerPoint that can help them properly format their slide decks. The next sections of this chapter cover slide deck designs and the additional features of PowerPoint that can make your slides effective and accessible for all virtual event participants.

## Designing Your Slides

The most often cited design principle for slides is either the rule of 7 or the 6-by-6 rule. The premise for these design guides is that slides are more effective with fewer words. The rule of 7 specifies that each slide should contain no more than 7 lines with 7 words per line. The slides should have no full sentences or paragraphs unless sharing a quote. The 6-by-6 rule follows that same goal, except it specifies only 6 lines and 6 words per line. Regardless of which design principle you follow, your goal should always be to include more visuals than words on your slides.

Suggestions for slide design include the following.

- Use a visual theme for your slideshow. However, assure that you are using contrasting colors. When you click on a theme in PowerPoint, for example, you can also select from additional color combinations. You should pay close attention to the colors displayed in order to make sure you have adequate color contrast. Another important feature of PowerPoint is the ability to search for accessible themes simply by typing "accessible" into the search bar. One caution here, though, you need to check the fonts size carefully even in these accessible themes as occasionally they can be too small.
- Use contrasting colors and avoid black and white only (for additional information regarding contrasting colors, visit https:// webaim.org/resources/contrastchecker/).
- Use color choices that complement your presentation.
- Be selective in your choice of clip art as most people have seen it if it is part of PowerPoint.
- Use animation only if needed to make a point.
- When using graphics, make them large enough to be easily read.
- Number each slide.
- Use only one slide per idea.
- Use lists. When you create lists, use the bulleted or numbered list formatting tool. This process allows a screen reader to identify the number of items in a list before it begins to read the items.

- Use properly formatted tables. The relationship between the cells is not defined if the table is not formatted correctly. Make sure to identify any header rows or columns (those cells that act as labels for the data within the table).

These suggestions are not all-inclusive but merely provide some design tips to assist you with the basics. However, the next section will address ways to ensure your slides are accessible to your participants. Virtual presenters and facilitators need to be concerned about accessibility whether or not they ask participants to complete a preregistration form that specifically seeks that information.

Accessibility in design is important for participants with audio processing and vision issues as well as people who are color-blind.

Visually impaired participants use screen readers to help them see the virtual event. Therefore, your design principles must ensure that your visuals can be read by screen readers and that the information obtained from your visuals with these tools encompasses the entirety of your virtual presentation, webinar, or e-meeting. Participants with auditory processing disorders need to be able to see and read everything that is occurring during your virtual event. Therefore, live captioning or the use of a sign language interpreter for the virtual event is needed. Also, if you elect to show video clips from the Internet, you need to be sure those videos have closed captioning capabilities. If you are using a YouTube video, for example, you may turn on the closed captioning option; however, the transcript often contains errors. You cannot assume because a video has closed captioning that the information provided will be 100 percent perfect. You can, however, edit the automatic closed captioning to correct mistakes or you can add your own captioning if you desire.

If you choose to show websites during your presentation, check those sites for accessibility. If you have questions about a website and its accessibility, you can visit the W3C site for further explanation: www.w3.org/standards/webdesign/accessibility.

PowerPoint has a built-in accessibility checker that can be of assistance to you; however, even the best accessibility checker will occasionally miss some of the issues. For this reason, you must manually review your materials as well.

The PowerPoint Accessibility Checker uses a set of rules for identifying issues that may be problematic for people with disabilities. Your PowerPoint file goes through a verification process and any issues uncovered by the accessibility checker are marked according to severity as follows: error, warning, tip, or intelligent services.

- **Error:** If you have any content that people with disabilities would have difficulty reading or understanding (e.g., images with no alt text), the accessibility checker will mark it as error.
- **Warning:** If any of your content would render the document difficult (or impossible) to understand for people with disabilities (e.g., table has merged or split cells), the accessibility checker will mark it as warning (Center for Persons with Disabilities 2019).
- **Tip:** If any of your content could be presented in a different way and improve the user's experience, the accessibility checker will mark it as a tip. In these cases, people with disabilities have no problem understanding your content. The accessibility checker simply believes it could be improved upon for better understanding.
- **Intelligent services:** In this instance, your content has automatically been made accessible by artificial intelligence; however, it is tagged as intelligent services to indicate that you should review it for accuracy and context.

While the accessibility checker is an important part of the PowerPoint program, it does not have the capability of catching every issue. As mentioned previously, you must also manually review your slides for any potential issues. In particular, the accessibility checker does not or cannot perform the following tasks.

1. Determine proper read order.
2. Identify when a slide title is not the first item in the read order.
3. Identify when the alt text for an image is inaccurate or nonsensical.
4. Check for poor color contrast or inappropriate use of color.
5. Identify lists that are not formatted as lists.
6. Flag text that may be too small and/or difficult to read.

The following tips will help you design your PowerPoint slides and help you ensure that your virtual event is accessible to all.

- Use a sans serif font (e.g., Arial).
- Use a large font size (minimum of 20 point).
- Provide alternative text descriptions for all images, pictures, clipart, and graphics, and embed alt text descriptions in all images, photographs, clipart, graphics, maps, and charts. In PowerPoint, when alt text is added to an image you will not see it. So, if you want to check that an image has alt text, follow the steps for adding alt text. If alt text is present, you will be able to see it in the description pane.
- Avoid adding text boxes to slides; use the design features provided by PowerPoint.
- Avoid putting text over images; text on slides should have nothing behind it (no watermarks or images).
- Avoid using color to convey meaning.
- Use side titles. Every slide in a PowerPoint presentation should have a unique title. If you duplicate slide titles, you will confuse your viewers and make finding specific information too difficult. People using assistive technology such as screen readers will navigate by slide title.
- Use videos or video clips that are captioned and have audio description. Remember that most virtual platform for meetings and presentations do not offer real-time captioning. For now, though, captioning services must be paid for as an add-on for virtual events.

Once you have navigated the design process and determined that all of your materials for your virtual event, including the event itself, are accessible to any participant, you want to next practice giving your presentation or facilitating your webinar or e-meeting with the following guidelines. When presenting or facilitating, you should:

- Describe images and graphics to help those who are visually impaired or who do not have a good view of the screen better understand what you are discussing.

- Read the text on the slide and not rely on the participants to both read the text and listen to you at the same time.
- Repeat questions that are posed in the chat area before you answer them because not every participant can see them or follow them during the event.

At the start of your actual virtual event, you need to take some extra time to complete the following housekeeping duties.

- Disable any entry and/or exit tones that sound when participants come into and leave the event.
- Arrive at your virtual event approximately 15 minutes early and engage with participants who are also early.
- Explain how the question-and-answer session will be handled— whether you will ask for questions to be posted in the chat area or if you will allow participants to use their microphones.
- Explain how participants can access materials for your virtual event (i.e., handouts, websites); uploading them and pushing them out to participants rather than using screen sharing helps to conserve bandwidth and provides a higher-quality experience for participants.
- Explain how participants can access live captioning or a recording of the virtual event at its conclusion.
- Ask participants to shut down any other applications currently running on their computers, tablets, or smartphones.

Once these start-up duties are complete and you begin your virtual event, remember the following steps.

1. Create a relaxed atmosphere.
2. Do not attempt to serial process. A serial process is sequential, one process after the other; a parallel process is simultaneous, with numerous processes occurring concurrently (Serial vs. Parallel Process 2018). In the virtual event world, serial processing will create a backlog because the presenter or facilitator can handle only one step or item at a time and cannot move forward with the next step

or item until that first one is completed. Parallel processing allows for the virtual environment to work at its optimum. You have many parts working simultaneously—that is, the chat area for Q&A while you are polling your participants—to help you reach the ultimate conclusion.

3. Follow a speaking rhythm (speak, pause, prepare, act, and speak again).
4. Close your presentation to meet your objectives.

Give your participants an opportunity to interact on a regular basis, approximately every 5 to 7 minutes. You can have them engage in the following activities: polls, questions for the chat/Q&A area, games, setting status, and whiteboards, among others. Be sure to acknowledge participants' responses and incorporate them into your presentation, webinar, or e-meeting. Do not have them complete a poll or some other activity just for the sake of interactivity. Make the process worthwhile.

> At the end of your virtual event, you should feel a sense of accomplishment, but your participants should be energized and enthusiastic.

Adherence to design principles for your event materials and presentation/facilitation process means that every participant was able to gain something from your virtual event. Remember that accommodation is not the same as accessibility. Every virtual event should be accessible to any person wishing to participate, and no individual should have to ask for an accommodation to gain access.

Just because you bid adieu to your participants at the end of the virtual event does not mean you have nothing further to do. The last step in the virtual event planning and delivery process is that of follow-up. The final chapter in this text addresses the steps you should take to effectively conclude your event.

## References

Center for Persons with Disabilities. 2019. "PowerPoint Accessibility," WebAIM. https://webaim.org/techniques/powerpoint/.

Serial vs. Parallel Process. 2018. "Xait Blog." https://www.xait.com/resources/blog/serial-vs-parallel-process/.

# CHAPTER 5

# The Follow-Up to Virtual Presentations

When you complete your virtual presentation, webinar, or e-meeting, you really are not finished with your virtual event. Anyone who has ever facilitated a training session or engaged in a sales presentation, or teachers who have taught a class to completion, knows that the final step involves evaluation. Did you deliver training in a manner that resulted in the acquisition of knowledge, skills, and abilities? Did you interest the audience in your product or service with your sales presentation? Did your students learn the material they were supposed to learn?

Summative evaluations are the preferred method of ascertaining responses to the previous questions.

A summative evaluation is a method for assessing the effectiveness of an event such as a training session, class, or presentation to determine whether it should be continued or revised for improvement.

You also can use session, presentation, or student evaluations to capture the essence of value the participants ascribed to your virtual event. If you have attended traditional conferences or conventions, you often receive a session evaluation that you are asked to complete at the end of a presentation. Questions on that evaluation are generally created with Likert-scale response choices. You select 1 if you found the presentation to be of no value, 5 if you found it be exceptionally valuable, and numbers 2, 3, and 4 simply offer you options for more moderate responses. You may also find an open-ended question or two on that evaluation attempting to elicit ideas for session topics or presenters for the next year's conference. The goal of the session evaluations is to gather data that has relevance to the presenter and to the conference organization, data that reveals whether the presenter did a good job, had an interesting topic for the presentation, and whether the association chose wisely in having this person on the program.

Virtual events also typically use some type of evaluation designed to gain similar types of data. As a presenter or facilitator for a virtual event, you want to know if you hit all the marks you set for yourself at the outset of the event. Did participants enjoy the session? Do they have any suggestions for improvements?

The roadblock to evaluation of your virtual event is the very nature of the platform itself. In a traditional presentation, you ask attendees to complete the session evaluation at the end of the presentation. Depending on how the convention is managed, though, the presenter may not receive the completed evaluations at that point. A report may be forthcoming from the convention director at some specified date. Regardless of how the data is reported, the ease with which completed evaluations can be obtained in a traditional setting contrasts with the difficulties inherent in getting the same type of completed evaluation in the virtual environment.

> One way to make collection of your session evaluation data an easier, more manageable process is to create your evaluation instrument and have it ready for online completion at the end of your virtual event.

Before signing off the presentation, webinar, or e-meeting, you can ask participants to visit the link you push out in the chat area to complete the event evaluation. If you explain the importance of that data to you—how it drives what you do for future virtual events—perhaps they will take the few minutes needed to complete it. You certainly stand a better chance of getting that evaluation completed at the close of your event.

Some presenters will wait until the end of the event and then send thank-you e-mails to participants. Embedded in that message is a link to the event evaluation. If you do not delay in sending the thank-you message—send it within 24 hours of the completion of the virtual event—you will get a better completion rate for the evaluation. People generally handle requests for completion of event evaluations or surveys at the time of the event. Giving them additional time away from the event means the likelihood of completion declines. Therefore, I suggest that you have your survey instrument (questionnaire/evaluation) ready to deploy at the close of your virtual event.

Additional types of follow-up may be required at the close of your virtual event. If you established a registration process for your event, you may have some participants who registered but were unable to attend or were *no shows* at the actual event. You should send follow-up e-mails to those registered participants who did not attend, thank them for registering for the event, and tell them they were missed. Give them a link to the recording of your event and send any handouts as well. You never know why someone failed to show up at your virtual event, so be kind. You spend just a few minutes writing the message and attaching the handout(s), but you may gain participants for future events. People always remember kindness and generosity. End your event the way you began—with the audience needs in mind.

# CHAPTER 6

# Facilitating E-Meetings: A Different Type of Virtual Presentation

The previous chapters in this book have mentioned e-meetings as examples of virtual events. While many of the steps we have covered regarding planning and delivering virtual presentations apply to e-meetings, we would be remiss if we did not address the specifics of planning and facilitating e-meetings.

We live in a time where businesses have satellite offices and employees scattered across the globe, and we know that those businesses have had to find and use the most efficient means available to meet with employees or to have employees engage with one another as members of a team, task force, or committee. In the early stages, companies relied on travel to and from the home office to meet the needs of remote employees and the satellite facilities. However, they were never pleased with the amount of time an employee spent away from his or her job or with the cost of the travel (e.g., airline fees, hotel costs, per diem expenses for food). Therefore, meetings were scheduled very infrequently and only when necessary. Most often, business was conducted via telephone conference.

You may remember or can find examples of audio conferences in the business environment. The earliest image most likely will be that of a large conference table with numerous individuals seated around it and a speaker or two placed in convenient locations on the table. The individual in charge of the meeting initiated the phone call and turned on the speakers so that everyone could hear and participate in the meeting. You had the person to whom you were speaking on one end of the phone call and the members of the group who were participating in the audio conference on the other end. Looking back at my job search process at the end of my doctoral program, I remember participating in a few of these conference call pre-interviews. Trying to remember whose voice belonged to whom created more anxiety for me than did answering the questions posed to me. I had never met these individuals and had no frame of reference for them other than the organization where they were employed.

Moving forward about 25 years, we can see that audio conferences are still alive and well. However, advancements in technology have made it easier to connect from anywhere at any time. We no longer need to have the participants in one or two locations. In effect, the conference room has evolved into the conference call.

The focus of this chapter is e-meetings, so why are we looking at audio/video conferences? The evolution of audio conferencing has certainly given us choices. We can choose to hold meetings via a specific platform on the Internet or through an audio conference program. We do not want to discount the continued use of conference calls as many companies continue to use them. Also, as you will learn from reading the remainder of this chapter, many of the advantages and disadvantages associated with e-meetings are not impacted by the choice of platform or environment.

Moreover, audio conferences were the gateway for e-meetings. Virtual meeting platforms developed in response to a need. Companies had employees scattered across the globe and across time zones, and the use of audio or conference calling was not meeting their needs, especially for teams. Therefore, web conferencing programs were developed to address these needs.

As we considered previously, companies initially adopted virtual events as a cost-saving measure because they did not have to pay for travel costs for employees. However, because this chapter specifically focuses on e-meetings, we will review the pros and cons of them here. Some may be repetitive as they may apply to virtual events in general.

| Pros of E-Meetings | Cons of E-Meetings |
| --- | --- |
| No travel costs are required for attending e-meetings | Need to navigate multiple time zones |
| Affordable e-meeting programs are available | Technical difficulties keep participants from engaging at full capacity |
| Can be held anywhere you have an Internet connection (great for employees who are on the road handling sales and other duties) | Connection issues create problems for participants when attempting to use free Wi-Fi or smartphone service |

| Pros of E-Meetings | Cons of E-Meetings |
|---|---|
| Bring people together who would normally be unable to meet one another (build engagement, trust, and candor among teams) | Difficult to decipher body language cues |
| No lost productivity for employees who would ordinarily have to be out of the office and traveling for a traditional meeting | Cannot manage participants' distractions |

The biggest disadvantage of any virtual event is participants' distractions. Even in the conference calling world, participants are prone to doing other things: completing projects/work, sending e-mail, eating or making food, texting, checking social media, playing video games, and shopping online. Using e-meeting programs results in the same distractions—and perhaps more if your participants have a dual-monitor setup. So, how can we deal with those distractions especially since we cannot see what our e-meeting participants are doing on their end?

## How to Conduct an Effective E-Meeting

Virtual or e-meetings have become the most effective way for teams to stay connected. Even with the advancements in programs and platforms designed specifically for virtual meetings, we still want to facilitate these meetings in the same manner as traditional, on-site meetings. As mentioned in an earlier chapter, people believe that simply changing platforms—from face-to-face to virtual—does not mean that we should change any practices.

Unfortunately, if we continue to attempt the same processes in our e-meetings as we do in our on-site meetings, we encourage distractions, perhaps even promote them.

If we want to add value to our e-meetings, we need to do the following:

**Create and Publish an Agenda**. An agenda is the guide or road map for your meeting. When you create your agenda ahead of time and share it with your meeting participants, you give them the opportunity to prepare for each topic. Participation increases when people have time to think about a topic before being expected to express thoughts and opinions.

An agenda does not need to be lengthy. The concise approach is best. You do not want to include amounts of time you will allot to each topic on the agenda that you disseminate to participants. You cannot be sure how participants are going to react and whether they will share numerous thoughts and ideas or proffer only a few brief comments. You as the facilitator of the e-meeting can indicate approximate time for each topic on your own copy of the agenda; but as a rule of thumb, you should plan for 20 percent more time for each topic than what you believe you will need (Axtell 2016).

In selecting topics for your e-meeting, we want to answer each of the following questions before creating your agenda.

1. Why do we need this topic on our agenda?
2. How much time do we need to allot to this topic?
3. Where do we want to be at the end of our discussion on this topic?
4. What do we need our participants to do? (Axtell 2016)

Once you have your topics determined, you want to consider which participant should lead or guide each topic. You want to involve participants in the e-meeting, so you should let them know when you distribute the agenda that you want broad participation from the group. Since your participants will have the "heads up" that you are going to expect participation, they will be ready to respond when you strategically call on them to share what they think about a specific topic. As the facilitator, you should identify which participant aligns best with which topic before the e-meeting begins. This information does not need to be shared and is for your use only. You want your participants to prepare for the entire agenda.

Because you want broad participation and you want to ensure that every person gets the opportunity to express his or her views, you must not rush through the agenda. Plan for more time—as mentioned earlier, add 20 percent more time for each item. If you do not need the time, you can always end the e-meeting earlier than expected. However, you are better off having too much time scheduled for the e-meeting than not enough time.

Phillips suggests the following meeting lengths for specific meeting types (Phillips 2018).

| Meeting Type | Ideal Meeting Length |
|---|---|
| Regular team meeting | 15–30 minutes |
| Decision-making meeting | Few hours; possibly a full day |
| Brainstorming meeting | 40 minutes to 1 hour |
| Retrospective meeting | 30 minutes for every week in the project |
| One-on-one meeting | 30 minutes to 1 hour |
| Strategy meeting | 60–90 minutes |

Obviously, these suggested meeting lengths. Each facilitator must determine his or her own timeline depending on the agenda and the topics to be covered during the e-meeting.

In addition to the topics for the e-meeting agenda, you want to establish meeting guidelines—the expectations of participants in the e-meeting. As the facilitator, you want your participants to know what you want them to do. For example, do you want to allow every participant to speak freely or do you want to call on individual participants for contributions? Do you want all participants to turn on their web cameras and leave them on for the duration of the e-meeting? Or, do you just want the facilitator's web camera to be on? Should participants mute their microphones during the e-meeting, only unmuting them when they need to ask a question or contribute to the discussion?

Another way the facilitator can use the guidelines to help ensure an effective e-meeting is to ask participants to test their technology (e.g., web camera, audio, Wi-Fi). Many programs prompt participants to run an audio/video setup to ensure that everything is working. Encourage participants to use those tools. You can reduce a lot of anxiety by asking participants to handle these checks before the start of the e-meeting.

Establishing a clear agenda and guidelines for participants will help ensure your e-meeting progresses as planned. You should share the agenda and guidelines with participants at least 24 hours in advance of the e-meeting so they have sufficient time to familiarize themselves with the topics to be covered and with the requirements for participating.

**Focus on Relationships**. This item may seem the antithesis for running an effective meeting. However, setting aside time to build relationships is important to the overall success of your e-meeting. We should set aside the first part of our e-meeting to allow participants to connect with each other. They will want to catch up on life details. Best practice for the focus on relationship time is to set the e-meeting platform or program to open a minimum of 10 minutes early. The facilitator of the e-meeting should be present to greet people as they join the meeting. Encourage participants to show up early and speak with each other during this pre-meeting period.

Another way to focus on relationships in your e-meetings is for the facilitator to use participants' names when referring to them and their comments. People like hearing their names and appreciate being recognized. The use of names in an e-meeting helps build the sense of community necessary for success.

Therefore, before the e-meeting begins, you should first introduce every participant or have every participant introduce himself or herself.

**Start E-Meetings on Time**. Yes, in the previous section, we just reviewed the need for networking for participants in e-meetings. However, you still must begin the e-meeting on time. A delay in starting an e-meeting leads to annoyance on the part of your participants. This annoyance can filter into the actual e-meeting and result in fewer ideas, decreased morale, and overall crankiness of participants.

**Facilitate to Accomplish E-Meeting Goals**. Most associations and organizations whose bylaws specify such use *Roberts Rules of Order* as the parliamentary authority for conducting their meetings (Robert 2011). If you are facilitating an e-meeting for a company, though, the likelihood of your using *Robert's Rules* or even knowing parliamentary procedures is slim. Most e-meetings in the workplace are related to company needs and are less formal in nature.

As the facilitator, you should review with participants how you plan to direct the e-meeting. As previously covered, nonverbal cues are limited in the virtual environment. Since we do not have a mechanism for determining if participants have questions or desire to make comments, we must establish some operating guidelines for the e-meeting.

We want to garner buy-in from our participants for the e-meeting guidelines, so we want them to assist in establishing them. We can put forward some suggestions but leave the discussion open for participants' ideas. Three areas a facilitator wants to address for participation include:

- Keeping the discussion on track and bringing people back to the topic at hand if they wander
- Involving every participant in the discussion even if that requires calling on different participants
- Asking that every participant turn off or remove any technology that may pose a distraction during the e-meeting

You can raise these issues and allow participants to flesh out the guidelines to their satisfaction so that you can ensure the e-meeting will work for everyone.

If you prefer, you can bring a list of requests to the e-meeting and simply ask permission of the participants to do the things necessary to keep the e-meeting on track and moving toward completion. For example, you may ask their permission to manage the time and focus of the conversation, to keep it on track and focused. Or, you may want to seek approval for asking specific participants to begin the discussion on certain agenda items. Your goal as a facilitator is to encourage participation from everyone and to complete the agenda during the time allotted. However, you want to ensure that everyone is understanding the information. As previously mentioned, you cannot see participants' faces to gauge their understanding or confusion, so you want to allow time for the discussion of each agenda item to ensure understanding by all.

**Prepare Participants to Actively Listen**. My university business communication classes always include a formal lesson on listening skills development. We want to help our students understand the connection between listening and communication. One of the first things we do in class is to discuss the following statement: "Listening and hearing are the same." I get a myriad of comments about how these two words are interchangeable and have essentially the same meaning. From that point, we move into a discussion on the definition of hearing. According to Merriam-Webster, hearing refers to "the process, function, or power of perceiving sound; *specifically*, the special sense by which noises and tones are received as stimuli" (Hearing 2019). I stress to my students that hearing refers to the physiological process that involves the ears and the recognition of sound or noise.

We then move to a discussion of the definition of listening. Merriam-Webster defines listen as "to pay attention to sound; e.g., *listen* to music; to hear something with thoughtful attention, to give thoughtful attention; e.g., *listen* to a plea; and to be alert to catch an expected sound; *listen* for her step" (Listen 2019). In all of these definitions, listening is explained as more than merely hearing a sound.

> Listening means paying attention to the sound and interpreting it for what the sound means.

Ever since we were babies and new to the world of sound, our perception has been that if we want to garner attention, we must make noise. So, we learned that the spoken word (or cries in the initial stages of life) gets us what we want. As time moved along, our belief that speaking was more important than listening was reinforced. Our teachers wrote our assignments on the board rather than repeat them numerous times when asked; then our teachers began handing out assignment sheets to avoid having to write anything on the board. Now, we have online classes and online assignment hubs where teachers provide the information that we need without the need for us to listen to instructions for assignments.

Our personal lives have fared no better. Once we were a vocal society, engaging with one another in conversation. Now we rely on our smartphones and texting to communicate with friends and family; even our business relationships are largely managed through text messaging and e-mails. Our interpersonal communication skills are abysmal and continue to deteriorate with every generation. In fact, the need for employees with excellent listening skills is beginning to appear frequently in job advertisements as a criterion for employment.

Therefore, as facilitators of e-meetings, we need to prepare participants to listen to the information being discussed. We can aim for active listening, the deep listening used by counselors and therapists. However, active listening relies on processing both the spoken words as well as the nonverbal communication generated by the speaker. In a virtual environment, the ability to see the body language of the speaker is almost impossible for the participants, especially if it involves anything other than affect displays and eye contact. So, what can facilitators of e-meetings do to encourage listening in their participants?

We have already covered a few of the items that are also paramount to encouraging participants to listen during the e-meeting: creating and sharing an agenda, networking, and finding the right environment for participating in the e-meeting. However, as the facilitator, you also want to consider the time you are setting the e-meeting. Another of my college professors from long years ago warned us never to show a video or video clip (in today's lingo, a YouTube clip) right after lunch unless you want to put your students or audience to sleep. When people have just completed a meal and the room is darkened to ensure the video is clearly visible, the likelihood of sleep invading their subconscious is virtually 100 percent.

Participating in e-meetings may not require an individual participant to have a darkened room, but certainly the time of day has an impact on the person's ability to listen and pay attention to the discussion. Oliver Staley, in his article in "Quartz at Work," reported the best time to meet is on Tuesday afternoon at 2:30—if you are looking for attendance. This information came from a study conducted by YouCanBookMe, a company in the United Kingdom that creates scheduling apps for businesses. The study resulted in over 2 million responses to 530,000 invitations (Staley 2016). However, if you are more concerned about performance (e.g., listening), you do not want to schedule your meetings in the afternoon.

Shai Danziger, Jonathan Levav, and Liora Avnaim-Pesso sought to determine the impact of time of day on decision making. They were looking at judges' decisions in parole hearings and whether those rulings were heavily dependent on the time of day the hearing was scheduled. Danziger and colleagues learned from their research that fatigue and behavior (e.g., hunger) have an impact on decision making. In fact, their findings revealed that if the judges were tired and/or hungry, they tended to make simple decisions. For prisoners involved in their study, Levav reported, that the closer the hearings were to a judge's break or lunch, the worse the outcome would be for the prisoners seeking parole. The judge defaulted to the most expedient decision—denial of parole (Danziger, Leva, and Avnaim-Pesso 2011).

If you are attempting to schedule an e-meeting that requires decision-making skills, you should attempt to hold them in the mornings when participants are fresh, usually between 9 a.m. and 11 a.m. Obviously, not every meeting can be scheduled during the morning hours, and you often must contend with time and dateline differences. However, if you must meet when participants are likely to be tired or hungry, you should attempt to avoid decisions, especially important decisions.

While you have more than one person in the e-meeting environment (unlike the judge making the parole decision in the study conducted by Danziger and colleagues), participants' decisions can still be impacted by groupthink. Merriam-Webster defines groupthink as "a pattern of thought characterized by self-deception, forced manufacture of consent, and conformity to group values and ethics" (Groupthink 2019). If participants are in a situation where they feel uncomfortable, are tired, and have not been actively listening, they are more likely to adopt the herd mentality and go with the decision put forward because it is the easiest and quickest way to end the e-meeting.

If we want our participants in our e-meeting to actively listen, we must prepare them to do so by ensuring that we set an optimum meeting time, that we allow them the opportunity prior to the start of the meeting to visit or network with one another, and that we encourage them to take handwritten notes.

As we will discuss in a later section on roles, having a participant serve as recorder or notetaker assures a written record of what occurred during the e-meeting. However, suggesting to participants to take notes for themselves can prove helpful to the listening process. Research supports that taking notes in longhand is advantageous.

Pam Mueller and Daniel Oppenheimer conducted research on the impact of laptops versus longhand in the acquisition of knowledge during classroom lectures and discussions. Their findings across three separate studies revealed that students who used laptops to take notes performed more poorly on conceptual questions than students who took notes in longhand. People who take notes via computers are prone to aim for verbatim transcription. One impact of attempting to capture every word uttered during the e-meeting, lecture, or discussion is that the listeners do not actually process the information they are collecting. They do not rephrase it or put it into their own words; therefore, the outcome is reflective of someone who did not actively listen during the session (Mueller and Oppenheimer 2014).

Again, we cannot force people to listen during an e-meeting. Distractions are all around us, and even when we ask participants to remove distractions or to turn off smartphones, laptops, and other devices, we cannot force them to do so. The next sections address ways in which we can further encourage participation and listening in our e-meetings, particularly the one regarding engagement. If participants understand that they are expected to engage in the discussion, to contribute ideas or thoughts, then they are much more likely to actively listen, to avoid distractions, and to be prepared to respond when addressed.

**Engage Participants Every 10 Minutes**. John Medina, a molecular biologist and author of *Brain Rules*, reports that the average attention span is 10 minutes (Medina 2014). By engaging with participants every 10 minutes, you can ensure that they are not distracted, bored, or on the verge of checking out of the e-meeting. As mentioned previously, you want to encourage participation from everyone. Therefore, engaging participants every 10 minutes is one way you can achieve both goals. You can use a round-robin approach and ask every participant to share an experience or insight related to the topic. Set a time limit of 5 minutes for each person so your more vocal extroverts do not overpower your introverts who are not as comfortable vocalizing their thoughts and ideas. If the group is too large for everyone to respond to each question, you can alternate calling on particular individuals for their input.

Other ways you can engage participants include asking them to write down questions they have during the meeting and collect the questions at the end, dividing participants into small groups and having them complete a task, or breaking the meeting into sections led by a different participant for each section. When participants are asked to write down their questions during the e-meeting, they are being given an opportunity to speak up. You can collect the questions and then read them aloud so that all participants get their concerns addressed. Also, you can break participants into groups and ask them to accomplish a small task or to reach a decision together. Once they have completed their task, you can ask each group to share the outcome with the entire group. Using different participants as presenters can be extremely helpful, especially in the active listening realm. Also, participants asked to handle different topics or parts of the agenda feel more connected to the material or project.

**Assign Role to Participants Before the E-Meeting Begins**. Most meetings of any type have a facilitator or leader and a recorder or secretary. The facilitator directs or leads the meeting, and the recorder or secretary takes the minutes or notes for the meeting. Again, only meetings governed by *Robert's Rules of Order* require the taking of minutes. For company-based meetings, the focus would be on taking notes.

As the facilitator, you can ask for a volunteer to take notes for the e-meeting or you can assign someone to take the notes. In face-to-face meetings, the facilitator or leader usually assigns roles to participants based on their strengths and weaknesses. For example, a participant who likes to speak out of turn or to interject unrelated information into the discussion would likely be asked to take notes for the meeting. By giving that individual a responsibility, he or she would be less likely to disrupt the meeting proceedings. In the e-meeting environment, you may choose someone who often engages in discussions to such an extent that others are unable to contribute. If you are unsure of the personalities of your participants, you may want to stay with the volunteer process and ask for someone to take the notes for the e-meeting. However, each participant needs some type of job (e.g., taking notes, managing the slideshow, writing down questions). Without clear individual responsibility, participant engagement suffers.

Most platforms and programs for e-meetings offer you the option to record the e-meeting. While you may think that the recording eliminates the need for handwritten notes, you may want to ask yourself who will transcribe the notes from the recording. Only one platform currently uses live captioning. So, unless your organization is using that platform, someone will need to view the recording and take notes for the e-meeting if you do not assign that task during the e-meeting.

Notes that are taken during an e-meeting can be shared with participants so that everyone has a record of what was discussed, what tasks were assigned (and to whom), and what the timeline for completion of any projects encompassed. Also, any discrepancies in the notes can be addressed and corrected based on input from participants. No one is 100 percent accurate in notetaking unless that person is a certified court reporter whose job is to take verbatim testimony. Therefore, asking participants to review a copy of the notes created by the designated notetaker for the e-meeting is a good method for ensuring accuracy of information.

If you follow these suggestions, you should be able to facilitate an e-meeting to its conclusion with the requisite input from participants allowing for the agenda to be fully addressed and plans established for next steps. However, you need to close the e-meeting before you can say that everything went as planned.

## How to Close an E-Meeting

Once the e-meeting has ended, you have a few steps to take to ensure that participants leave with a clear purpose.

Send thank-you message to participants and include a link to the recording for the e-meeting. While you may think this an unnecessary step since the participants were present at the e-meeting, the idea is that participants who work remotely or as part of the globally distributed workforce may wish to revisit some of the issues discussed during the e-meeting or need clarification on a topic or decision. In addition, if you had people who were unable to attend the e-meeting, sending them a link to the recording assists them with getting up to speed on what was discussed and what the next steps involve.

If there are action items or projects for follow-up, assign those to specific participants. You also will want to set deadlines for these items or projects. In addition, if during the e-meeting you had items that arose as part of side discussions that you tabled, you want to make sure that participants are reminded of them and let them choose the next steps for those (Phillips 2018).

Axtell posited that meetings fail because facilitators fail to close properly. He suggested the following essential tasks that must be handled to ensure the conversation or meeting is closed (Axtell 2015):

**Seek clarification of understanding before changing topics**: Don't assume that everyone understands the topic until we secure their response to the question "Does anyone have anything else to add or any questions before we move to the next topic?"

**Check for participants' agreement with decisions:** Ensure that all participants agree with the decisions made in the e-meeting. Ask if everyone is on board with the decision or with where we are going. If a participant is not, then address his or her concerns and answer questions so that the situation can be resolved.

**Agree on what is to take place after the e-meeting:** The facilitator needs to get firm commitments as to who will be responsible for the next steps and by what deadlines those steps need to be completed. Agree on a clearly defined action plan complete with next steps, a timeline, and specific tasks to be completed (and the participants charged with completing them) before the next meeting.

**Do not forget about feedback:** The follow-up process was discussed in a previous chapter. However, as part of e-meetings, we want to ask for anonymous feedback from time to time to learn how effective the e-meeting was from our participants' perspective. The evaluation does not have to be lengthy, perhaps two or three questions such as the following.

- Was the e-meeting meaningful to you?
- How would you improve the e-meeting?
- Was the e-meeting a valuable use of your time?
- What worked today that we should continue?
- What did not work today that we should change, eliminate, or improve?

You do not want your e-meetings to be viewed as wasteful, not needed, not engaging, or inefficient. Therefore, the only way to gauge the effectiveness of the e-meeting is to ask participants for their evaluation. If time permits, schedule one-on-one meetings with participants to gain their insights on how to improve the e-meetings. Also, if possible, create an online space—a feedback area (e.g., a virtual suggestion box)—where participants can share their thoughts, insights, and ideas after the e-meeting.

Throughout this chapter, we have discussed e-meetings from the perspective of the facilitator or leader. At this point, we need to add some etiquette tips for participants (Powers 2018) so that they are prepared to avoid the pitfalls that might create problems for them in the virtual environment.

## Virtual Meeting Etiquette Tips for Participants

In 16th-century Spain, the French word *étiquette* was altered to *etiqueta* and defined as "the written protocols describing orders of precedence and behavior demanded of those who appeared in court. Eventually, *etiqueta* came to be applied to the court ceremonies themselves as well as the documents which outlined the requirements for them" (Etiquette 2019). In today's vernacular, *etiquette* refers to procedures and behaviors dictated by authority or proper breeding that individuals must follow in social or official situations. While we may assume that no official guidelines dictate our behavior in e-meetings, we would be wrong in our assumption that we do not need to follow certain tenets of appropriate behavior. Some of the etiquette tips we will cover in the next section have previously been mentioned in other areas of this text. However, they bear repeating here.

**Be Aware of Your Background.** Choose the proper location for participating in the e-meeting. You do not want the other participants in the e-meeting to see an unmade bed, piles of dirty clothes or dishes, or stacks of papers or books on a sloppy desk. Also, check to make sure the lighting is appropriate. You do not want the room to be too bright or too dark.

**Wear Appropriate Attire.** Dress as you would for any face-to-face meeting with attention to color choices and patterns for clothing. You want to wear clean clothing and be properly groomed (e.g., no bed head or unkempt beards). Choose colors that are appropriate for video and avoid stripes, plaids, or any designs that create a halo or shimmery effect when viewed through a camera lens.

**Handle Distractions Before the E-Meeting Starts.** Turn off smartphones, tablets, other computers, televisions, stereos, and any other voice-activated technologies. Also, if you have pets, particularly dogs, remove them from the environment where you will be participating in the e-meeting. If you have children, make sure they are not in the room and cannot enter the room while you are participating in the e-meeting. Avoid using your keyboard to type notes or any other materials during the e-meeting because the sound can be distracting to other participants.

**Use Your Voice Appropriately When Contributing to the E-Meeting.** While technology has improved the sound quality in the virtual environment, you still need to speak clearly, concisely, and slowly, especially if participants may not be familiar with your dialect. You want to ensure that all participants can understand you. Your normal speaking voice should be fine, so you should not need to yell.

**Do Not Eat during the E-Meeting**. Participants can hear you chewing even if they cannot see you eating. If your e-meeting uses video technology and everyone is visible, you do not want your co-participants to have to watch you eat.

**Make Eye Contact When Possible (or When Applicable) during the E-Meeting**. If your facilitator uses the video component for the e-meeting and all participants are visible, you want to make sure when you are looking directly at the web cam when speaking. In a previous chapter, we examined nonverbal communication—eye contact, in particular—and learned that as participants in any virtual event, we should think of the web camera as our audience. So, for e-meetings, you want to do the same.

> Think of your web camera as the other participants in the e-meeting. Visualize them through the camera lens.

**Do Not Perform Other Tasks While in the E-Meeting**. In the previous section, we discussed the importance of removing all distractions from the environment before the start of the e-meeting. Hopefully that means you will have eliminated any jobs or projects you are involved in or working with as well. You cannot listen effectively or participate actively in an e-meeting if you allow yourself to work on other things—and that includes e-mail, text messages, and social media posts.

**Do Not Forget about the Mute Button**. Occasionally, you may find that the background noise gets overwhelming. The noise can result from feedback from conflicting microphones or location sounds (e.g., coffee shop noise, airport announcements). Keep your microphone muted unless and until you need to or desire to speak.

**Practice Patience during the E-Meeting**. Not everyone has the same bandwidth or connectivity, so a delay in response may be the fault of technology more than the person. Be patient and allow a few seconds to pass. The participant may simply be trying to figure out how to unmute himself or herself. When in doubt, be kind and practice patience.

Helping participants prepare for an e-meeting is the job of a savvy facilitator. Also, helping participants to understand that the rules of etiquette apply in e-meetings as much as they do in any other environment is paramount to both facilitator and participant success. Sharing the guidelines above is the first step toward ensuring successful participation in any e-meeting. Help participants understand their roles in the e-meeting environment, and you will reap the rewards of positive feedback for your effective e-meeting.

At the end of the day—or at the end of the e-meeting—you want your participants to exit the platform or program with a clear objective. You want them to feel inspired, not frustrated. Facilitating a successful e-meeting can seem a daunting task. However, if you prepare yourself with the guidelines set forth in this chapter, you can be confident of success. You can turn passive participants into active listeners. You can ensure that participants do not leave your e-meeting being unprepared for the next steps.

# References

Axtell, P. April 14, 2016. "What Everyone Should Know about Running Virtual Meetings," *Harvard Business Review*. https://hbr.org/2016/04/what-everyone-should-know-about-running-virtual-meetings.

Axtell, P. March 11, 2015. "The Right Way to End a Meeting," *Harvard Business Review*. https://hbr.org/2015/03/the-right-way-to-end-a-meeting.

Danziger, S., J. Leva, and L. Avnaim-Pesso. April 26, 2011. "Extraneous Factors in Judicial Decisions," *Proceedings of the National Academy of Sciences of the United States of America* 108, no. 17, pp. 6889–92. doi:10.1073/pnas.1018033108.

Etiquette. 2019. "Merriam-Webster." https://www.merriam-webster.com/dictionary/etiquette.

Groupthink. 2019. "Merriam-Webster." https://www.merriam-webster.com/dictionary/groupthink.

Hearing. 2019. "Merriam-Webster." https://www.merriam-webster.com/dictionary/hearing.

Listen. 2019. "Merriam-Webster." https://www.merriam-webster.com/dictionary/listening.

Medina, J. 2014. *Brain Rules*. Seattle, WA: Pear Press.

Mueller, P.A., and D.M. Oppenheimer. 2014. "The Pen is Mightier than the Keyboard: Advantages of Longhand over Laptop Note Taking." *Psychological Science*, pp. 1–10. doi:10.1177/0956797614524581.

Phillips, J. November 6, 2018. "How to Run Effective Meetings," *Slackhq*. https://slackhq.com/run-effective-meetings.

Powers, T. July 25, 2018. "The New Rules of Virtual Meeting Etiquette," Powers Resource Center. http://powersresourcecenter.com/the-new-virtual-meeting-etiquette/.

Robert, H.M. 2011. *Robert's Rules of Order Newly Revised*. 11th ed. http://www.robertsrules.com/history.html.

Staley, O. June 7, 2016. "The Best Day and Time to Hold a Meeting," *Quartz at Work*. https://qz.com/work/653033/heres-the-best-day-and-time-to-hold-a-meeting/.

# Conclusion

As technology continues to evolve and we see the growth of artificial intelligence and augmented reality, participation in the virtual environment is assured to grow. Knowing how to effectively manage virtual events—whether presentations, webinars, or e-meetings—is paramount to success in every industry. We cannot assume that the transfer of knowledge and skills from the traditional face-to-face to the virtual environment is as simple as turning on the web camera. The need for best practices should drive us to learn more and create strategies for delivering our virtual events.

In this book, we have looked at differences between virtual and traditional presentations, at the role nonverbal communication plays in virtual events, at the accessibility issues that must be considered when planning any virtual event, and finally at e-meetings and the guidelines and etiquette rules for effectively managing them. Each step of the way, we reviewed processes and procedures designed to improve our skills.

In the virtual world, we believe we are anonymous. We are not. What we do and say can have a profound impact on individuals who choose to be part of our presentations, webinars, and e-meetings. We should strive to give them our very best. Take the tools and techniques from this book and use them to deliver effective virtual presentations and to facilitate exceptional webinars and e-meetings. Be the person that participants want to see again in the virtual environment.

# Epilogue

My desire when I began to write this book was to create a product that would help people become more effective virtual presenters or facilitators of webinars and e-meetings. I hope this book helps you improve your skills. As you read through the chapters, I believe you will find some information that will be of benefit to you. However, I also believe in asking people to evaluate my work and to provide constructive feedback that will assist me in making improvements. I do this in my face-to-face classes by using a mid-term evaluation and in my online classes with a suggestion box. In both cases, students' anonymity is assured. Of course, I get the occasional outliers—I'm the best teacher ever! I am the worst teacher ever!—and have developed rather thick skin over my 24-year teaching career. I still seek the input of my students. I do not read Rate My Professor postings as I feel they do not get to the heart of the matter—the constructive suggestions that are applicable to my classes, the ways in which I can improve them. Those ideas from students are what I am seeking.

So, if you have any suggestions for modifications to this book—or for ways I can make it better—please contact me. I really do appreciate constructive feedback.

K. Virginia Hemby, PhD
Professor
Department of Marketing
Jennings A. Jones College of Business
Middle Tennessee State University
MTSU Box 40
Murfreesboro, TN 37132
+1 615 898 2369 (Office)
virginia.hemby-grubb@mtsu.edu

# Bibliography

AMA Staff. 2011. "Perfect Your Virtual Presentations." https://www.ama-net.org/training/articles/perfect-your-virtual-presentations.aspx.

American Management Association. 2019. https://www.amanet.org/.

Axtell, P. April 14, 2016. "What Everyone Should Know about Running Virtual Meetings," *Harvard Business Review*. https://hbr.org/2016/04/what-everyone-should-know-about-running-virtual-meetings.

Axtell, P. March 11, 2015. "The Right Way to End a Meeting," *Harvard Business Review*. https://hbr.org/2015/03/the-right-way-to-end-a-meeting.

Center for Persons with Disabilities. 2019. "PowerPoint Accessibility," WebAIM. https://webaim.org/techniques/powerpoint/.

Danziger, S., J. Leva, and L. Avnaim-Pesso. April 26, 2011. "Extraneous Factors in Judicial Decisions." *Proceedings of the National Academy of Sciences of the United States of America* 108, no. 17, pp. 6889-92. doi:10.1073/pnas.1018033108.

Darlin, D. June 26, 2014. "How the Future Looked in 1964: The Picturephone," *The New York Times, March of Progress*. https://www.nytimes.com/2014/06/27/upshot/how-the-future-looked-in-1964-the-picturephone.html.

Etiquette. 2019. "Merriam-Webster." https://www.merriam-webster.com/dictionary/etiquette.

Global Research and Insights. August, 2018. "Beyond Millennials: The Next Generation of Learners," Pearson. https://www.pearson.com/content/dam/one-dot-com/one-dot-com/global/Files/news/news-announcements/2018/The-Next-Generation-of-Learners_final.pdf.

Groupthink. 2019. "Merriam-Webster." https://www.merriam-webster.com/dictionary/groupthink.

Hearing. 2019. "Merriam-Webster." https://www.merriam-webster.com/dictionary/hearing.

Listen. 2019. "Merriam-Webster." https://www.merriam-webster.com/dictionary/listening.

Medina, J. 2014. *Brain Rules*. Seattle, WA: Pear Press.

*Meetings Today*. 2013. "Virtual Event Definitions." https://www.meetingstoday.com/magazines/article-details/articleid/19191/title/virtual-event-definitions.

Mueller, P.A., and D.M. Oppenheimer. 2014. "The Pen Is Mightier than the Keyboard: Advantages of Longhand over Laptop Note Taking." *Psychological Science*, pp. 1-10. doi:10.1177/0956797614524581.

Novak, M. 2013. "Future Calling: Videophones in the World of the Jetsons." https://www.smithsonianmag.com/history/future-calling-videophones-in-the-world-of-the-jetsons-6789346/.

Owen, A. August 28, 2018. "The History and Evolution of the Smartphone: 1992–2018." https://www.textrequest.com/blog/history-evolution-smartphone/.

Pew Research Center: Internet and Technology. February 5, 2018. "Mobile Fact Sheet." http://www.pewinternet.org/fact-sheet/mobile/.

Phillips, J. November 6, 2018. "How to Run Effective Meetings," *Slackhq*. https://slackhq.com/run-effective-meetings.

Powers, T. July 25, 2018. "The New Rules of Virtual Meeting Etiquette," Powers Resource Center. http://powersresourcecenter.com/the-new-virtual-meeting-etiquette/.

Robert, H.M. 2011. *Robert's Rules of Order Newly Revised*. 11th ed. http://www.robertsrules.com/history.html.

Serial vs. Parallel Process. 2018. "Xait Blog." https://www.xait.com/resources/blog/serial-vs-parallel-process/.

Staley, O. June 7, 2016. "The Best Day and Time to Hold a Meeting," *Quartz at Work*. https://qz.com/work/653033/heres-the-best-day-and-time-to-hold-a-meeting/.

# APPENDIX 1

# Checklist for Virtual Event

| Time | Task | Done? |
|------|------|-------|
| 30 minutes prior | Log-in to platform/program | |
| 30 minutes prior | Ensure audio/video is working and recording functional | |
| 30 minutes prior | Upload and run "cycle slides" (if applicable) | |
| 20 minutes prior | Ensure polling slides are created and loaded properly | |
| 20 minutes prior | Check that other visuals or applications as necessary are ready to go | |
| 15 minutes prior | Make announcement to let participants know 15 minutes until start time; ask them to check audio/video | |
| 10 minutes prior | Meet and greet participants as they arrive for event; allow participants to network with each other (e-meeting) | |
| 1 minute prior | Hit "record" | |
| Showtime | Introduction | |
| | Deliver your presentation or webinar/facilitate e-meeting | |
| | Monitor time | |
| | Monitor question-and-answer box, choose questions, and answer the easy ones | |
| | Introduce question-and-answer | |
| | Check for audience questions, and use prepared or planted questions to jump-start the session if necessary | |
| | Close presentation | |
| | Ask participants to complete evaluation form (push out via virtual platform or provide link) | |
| | Turn off recording | |
| | Copy question-and-answer log (if applicable) to the platform | |
| | Save presentation with polling data and annotations (if applicable) to the platform | |
| 5 minutes after | Close the platform; end virtual event | |

# APPENDIX 2

# Self-Evaluation Form for Virtual Presentation

| Action item | Did you achieve your goal? | How do you know? | Maintain, delete, or improve | Specific steps to improve performance |
|---|---|---|---|---|
| **Step 1. Identify your objectives and outcomes** | | | | |
| Clearly defined my purpose for the presentation | | | | |
| Got buy-in from all stakeholders | | | | |
| Clearly defined the outcome | | | | |
| Final presentation was geared to that outcome | | | | |
| **Step 2. Learn the platform** | | | | |
| Platform or program was appropriate for my purposes | | | | |
| Able to use all the appropriate functions comfortably | | | | |
| Platform or program was appropriate for my audience | | | | |
| No problems noted with audience connectivity | | | | |
| Used all functions appropriate for this virtual presentation | | | | |
| **Step 3. Create a project plan** | | | | |
| Roles and responsibilities were assigned properly | | | | |
| No problems were noted in meeting deadlines or assigned tasks | | | | |
| Plan is usable as-is for the next virtual presentation | | | | |

| Action item | Did you achieve your goal? | How do you know? | Maintain, delete, or improve | Specific steps to improve performance |
|---|---|---|---|---|
| **Step 4. Work with others** | | | | |
| Chose the appropriate people for assistance | | | | |
| Feedback was timely and useful | | | | |
| No problems noted with deadlines or quality of work | | | | |
| **Step 5. Create compelling content** | | | | |
| Invitation process got attendance numbers desired | | | | |
| Invitations were timely and went to correct people | | | | |
| Invitation gave specifics as to what to expect from virtual event | | | | |
| No problems with registration or log-in | | | | |
| Introduction was clear and focused on attaining outcome | | | | |
| Housekeeping details were appropriate and concise | | | | |
| Agenda was appropriate for the audience and outcome | | | | |
| Content was properly targeted to the participants | | | | |
| **Step 6. Create visuals that support your presentation** | | | | |
| Number of visuals was appropriate | | | | |
| Words in the visuals were all spelled correctly | | | | |
| Transitions, animations, and other visual aids worked properly | | | | |
| Pictures and clip art were appropriate for presentation and audience | | | | |
| Application sharing (if applicable) went smoothly | | | | |
| **Step 7. Sharpen your presentation skills** | | | | |
| Felt comfortable during the presentation | | | | |

| Action item | Did you achieve your goal? | How do you know? | Maintain, delete, or improve | Specific steps to improve performance |
|---|---|---|---|---|
| Transitions from one visual to the next were seamless | | | | |
| Appropriate level of interactivity with my audience | | | | |
| Asked questions and interacted with participants at optimal times | | | | |
| Displayed good vocal skills | | | | |
| **Step 8. Rehearse** | | | | |
| No unexpected challenges with the participants | | | | |
| Accurate feedback from participants | | | | |
| No unexpected problems or challenges appeared during rehearsal | | | | |
| Changes based on rehearsal were easy to make and did not create time pressure | | | | |
| **Step 9. Present and multitask effectively** | | | | |
| Appeared calm and stress-free during presentation | | | | |
| Did not lose my place or my concentration | | | | |
| Any problems were invisible to the audience | | | | |
| Question-and-answer session went as planned | | | | |
| Audience asked valid questions | | | | |
| Process of taking audience questions worked efficiently | | | | |
| Answers were targeted and concise | | | | |
| Sufficient time allotted for question-and-answer session | | | | |
| Call to action at end of presentation was clear | | | | |

| Action item | Did you achieve your goal? | How do you know? | Maintain, delete, or improve | Specific steps to improve performance |
|---|---|---|---|---|
| **Step 10. Follow up and keep learning** | | | | |
| Participants responded and took appropriate action | | | | |
| Thank-you letters went out in a timely fashion (within 24 hours of event) | | | | |
| "Sorry we missed you" letters went out in a timely fashion (within 24 hours of event) | | | | |
| Video recording of presentation was good quality | | | | |
| Recording was posted quickly, and links were included in all communication with registrants and participants (within 24 hours of event) | | | | |
| Evaluations created for event measured important data | | | | |
| Evaluations were sent out in a timely manner (or pushed out to participants at end of event) | | | | |
| Feedback from evaluations was useful and clear | | | | |
| Feedback from participants was positive | | | | |

# About the Author

**Dr K. Virginia Hemby-Grubb** is a professor in the Department of Marketing at Middle Tennessee State University. She earned a PhD in adult education, with a concentration in business from the University of Southern Mississippi in 1995. Dr Hemby-Grubb began her teaching career in the Technology Support and Training Department at Indiana University of Pennsylvania, Indiana, PA (1995 to 2004). She joined the Department of Marketing (formerly the Business Communication and Entrepreneurship Department) in the Jones College of Business at Middle Tennessee State University in August 2004. Dr Hemby-Grubb was the recipient of the John Robert Gregg Award in 2018, the Association for Research in Business Education—Delta Pi Epsilon National Leadership Award in 2016, and the National Business Education Association Teacher of the Year Award for Outstanding Contributions to Business Education by a Senior College or University Business Teacher in 2014. In 2011, she received the Distinguished Educator in Distance Learning Award from Middle Tennessee State University.

Dr Hemby-Grubb teaches the following graduate and undergraduate courses (online, hybrid, and/or traditional face-to-face classes): business communication; virtual business presentations; professional meeting, event, exhibition, and convention (MEEC) management; technology for the MEEC industry; career decision making; employment communication; and workplace etiquette and protocol. She has conducted research and delivered presentations in the area of virtual presentations as follows: Association for Business Communication, 81st Annual International Conference, Albuquerque, NM, *Presentation*: Teaching Virtual Presentation Skills: A Systematic Literature Review; 2016 Texas Career Education Summer Conference, Fort Worth Convention Center, Fort Worth, TX, *Presentation*: Virtual Presentations, e-Meetings, and Webinars: Teaching Technology-Driven Presentation Skills (virtual session); Mountain-Plains Business Education Conference (M-PBEA),

Albuquerque, NM, *Presentation*: Teaching Students Virtual Presentation Skills (virtual session); South Carolina Business Education Association (SCBEA) 2015 Conference, Columbia, SC, *Presentation*: Teaching Oral Presentation Skills in the Age of YouTube: Virtual Presentations, e-Meetings, and Webinars (virtual session); Oregon Business Education Association (OBEA) 2014 Conference, *Presentation:* Virtual Presentations, e-Meetings, and Webinars: Teaching Technology-Driven Presentation Skills (virtual session); Washington State Business and Marketing Pathway "Taking Charge of Change" 2014 Conference, Wenatchee, WA, *Presentation*: Virtual Presentations, e-Meetings, and Webinars: Teaching Oral Presentation Skills in the Age of YouTube (virtual session); National Business Education Association (NBEA) 2014 Annual Convention, Los Angeles, CA, *Presentation*: Virtual Presentations, e-Meetings, and Webinars—Presentations Now Require Skills Beyond PowerPoint; and 2014 Association for Business Communication Southeast Region Conference, Orlando, FL, *Presentation*: Teaching Oral Presentation Skills in the Age of YouTube: Virtual Presentations, and Business Communication.

Dr Hemby-Grubb has created courses for a concentration in MEEC management in the new tourism and hospitality management major as well as the sports, entertainment, and event (SEE) concentration in the marketing curriculum. While developing this program, Dr Hemby-Grubb has reviewed data related to the use of virtual meetings, conferences, and conventions and showed how the projected growth rate will affect MEEC managers who do not have the requisite skills in the virtual environment.

# Index

# OTHER TITLES IN OUR CORPORATE COMMUNICATION COLLECTION

Debbie DuFrene, Stephen F. Austin State University, *Editor*

- *Managerial Communication and the Brain: Applying Neuroscience to Leadership Practices* by Dirk Remley
- *Communicating to Lead and Motivate* by William C. Sharbrough
- *64 Surefire Strategies for Being Understood When Communicating with Co-Workers* by Walter St. John
- *Business Research Reporting* by Dorinda Clippinger
- *English Business Jargon and Slang: How to Use It and What It Really Means* by Suzan St. Maur
- *Conducting Business Across Borders: Effective Communication in English with Non-Native Speakers* by Adrian Wallwork
- *Strategic Thinking and Writing* by Michael Edmondson
- *Business Report Guides: Research Reports and Business Plans* by Dorinda Clippinger
- *Business Report Guides: Routine and Nonroutine Reports and Policies, Procedures, and Instructions* by Dorinda Clippinger
- *Managerial Communication For Organizational Development* by Reginald L. Bell and Jeanette S. Martin
- *Managerial Communication for Professional Development* by Reginald L. Bell and Jeanette S. Martin
- *Leadership Through A Screen: A Definitive Guide to Leading a Remote, Virtual Team* by Joseph Brady and Garry Prentice
- *New Insights into Prognostic Data Analytics in Corporate Communication* by Pragyan Rath and Kumari Shalini

## Announcing the Business Expert Press Digital Library

*Concise e-books business students need for classroom and research*

This book can also be purchased in an e-book collection by your library as

- *a one-time purchase,*
- *that is owned forever,*
- *allows for simultaneous readers,*
- *has no restrictions on printing, and*
- *can be downloaded as PDFs from within the library community.*

Our digital library collections are a great solution to beat the rising cost of textbooks. E-books can be loaded into their course management systems or onto students' e-book readers. The **Business Expert Press** digital libraries are very affordable, with no obligation to buy in future years. For more information, please visit **www.businessexpertpress.com/librarians**. To set up a trial in the United States, please email **sales@businessexpertpress.com**.

CPSIA information can be obtained
at www.ICGtesting.com
Printed in the USA
JSHW041158071220
10044JS00002B/41